ONE DAY AT A TIME

ONE DAY AT A TIME

The Story of My Life

BERNIE WINTERS

With Charmaine Carter

EBURY PRESS
London

Published in 1991 by Ebury Press
an imprint of the Random Century Group
Random Century House
20 Vauxhall Bridge Road
London SW1V 2SA

British Library Cataloguing-in-Publication Data
Winters, Bernie
One day at a time: The story of my life
I. Title
920

ISBN 0-09-175114-4

Typeset in Century Old Style from authors disk by Tek Art Ltd.,
Addiscombe, Croydon, Surrey

Printed and bound in Great Britain by Mackays of Chatham PLC, Kent

CONTENTS

Acknowledgements

So many people have been so helpful in putting this book together and Bernie and Charmaine would like particularly to thank Bob Monkhouse, Jimmy Tarbuck, Des O'Connor, Su Pollard, Leslie Crowther, Philip Jones, Maurice Leonard, Pete Murray, Johnny Riscoe, Lionel Blair, Cilla Black, and Peter Stringfellow. Special thanks, too, to Paddy Cutts, Pat Carter, Brian Klein, and Rowena Webb. Last, but by no means least, our thanks to Siggi, Ray and Tina Winters.

This life I have is all I have
And the life I have is yours
But the love I have for the life I have
Is yours and yours and yours.

Anon

I found this poem in an old book of Ronnie Corbett's at his house in Scotland. One night some years later I told it to Bernie, who loved it so much he adopted it as his own. I can see why: these few words encapsulate entirely his philosophy.

Jimmy Tarbuck

Dedication

My father was determined to finish this book at all costs. He even had the drafts read to him by both my wife Tina and his ghostwriter Charmaine at home at his bedside.

I hope, for his sake, that this book proves to be an inspiration to cancer patients and their families and friends.

Love you Mudge, Ray

Ray Winters

FOREWORD

WHEN George Gershwin died the great American novelist John O'Hara wrote, 'They tell me Gershwin's dead but I don't have to believe it if I don't want to.' They tell me Bernie Winters is dead. Not to me, he isn't. Not to his thousand friends or his million fans either. Bernie's more alive in our hearts and minds than most people who are still walking around.

Some people – most of them really – are difficult to recall in totality. You make an effort of memory and you conjure up a detail here, a detail there, the way someone laughed or the way they walked, their eyes perhaps or some odd saying they had. With Bernie, no effort is required. I just think of him and there's the entire man. I hear his voice and, more than that, I hear what he's saying. The huge, lovely presence of that personality is so strong that I can watch him walking up to me, feel his embrace, join in his laughter (of which there was a great deal) and share his tears (of which there were a great many).

Bernie's life force filled each minute of each day and imprinted itself on the minds of all who met him. You've heard the description 'larger than life'. Bernie's emotional and spiritual charge was just that, larger than life. That's why those who knew him know him still. He's going to be around as long as we are.

Great comedians are more than just funny. Mind you, Bernie was very funny indeed. Thirty years ago I remember watching him rehearse a couple of really rotten sketches for the ABC Television series he did with his brother Mike. I went outside and walked around the studio in Didsbury, Manchester – actually the old Odeon cinema – thinking what a terrible show it was that week and wondering if it would affect the audience's reaction to my own comedy spot.

When the show went on the air what had seemed glum stuff was transformed as magically as the Philosopher's Stone was meant to turn lead into gold, and I watched amazed and tried to understand how Bernie was doing it. This clown who had fretted and frowned and, agonised with nervous worry, drudged through that afternoon's rehearsals reciting and fluffing the witless lines – here he was, convulsing the crowd by making fun of the script, the show, the audience, his brother and himself. Mostly himself.

Bernie was doing then what I was to see him doing countless times after that extraordinary display of transforming tripe into treasure. Yes, of course he was using his professional skills – any good comic should be able to do that, but they won't necessarily do more than avert disaster when the material is as poor as this was. Bernie was stripping himself bare of all those vanities and pretensions that we humans tend to use in defensive situations. He made himself utterly vulnerable. Every look, every gesture, told the audience that he was helpless – he didn't know how he'd got into this mess, and please would they show mercy. He was endearing and comical and, more than anything else, a real human being evoking a real human response. It was great comedy from a performer capable of more than he ever really knew.

To say that Bernie led a modest life without vanity is to deny his pride in his family and friends, his home and his appearance (no performer was ever more immaculate); but deep within was an insecurity that took the form of natural modesty and a glorious capacity for self-mockery. Bernie's stories against himself, of his failures and mistakes, were – *are* – hilarious. On

TV chat shows with the likes of Terry Wogan, Des O'Connor and me he would tell tales of inadequacy that had us all weeping with laughter and affection. What made them so wonderful was that they came from the giant comic heart of Bernie – bitter humiliations and pain made jubilantly funny.

When the very new, very raw comedian met a very beautiful, very young dancer all those years ago their love affair could have been just one of those things. Somehow wisdom prevailed and Bernie became Bernie-and-Siggi.

Everyone in British show business knows Siggi. No performer's wife has ever been more fiercely loyal. My wife Jackie is loyal too, but not as fierce. Siggi brought to Bernie's existence the strength and discipline it needed. She has seldom suffered fools gladly and, where Bernie was sometimes too conciliatory, it was Siggi who had to cut through the thousand kinds of nonsense that waste a popular entertainer's time and money and get the important things done. If Bernie was the one who loved to say yes, she was the one who sometimes had to say no. In this way Siggi was able to give Bernie what he may have needed most. He needed to be loved. And, of course, he was and is.

When Siggi asked me to join Jimmy Tarbuck in speaking a few words of tribute at Bernie's funeral, I lay in bed the previous night and silently asked Bernie what I should say. He rolled his eyes to heaven in frustration and said, 'Listen to the man! Mr Words, doesn't know what to say! Bubbela, it's not an audition, the first of a series, the Palladium, is it? It's a freebie, you're doing it for friends, darling. I mean, if it was me having to speak at your funeral, we'd have a problem. I wouldn't 'ave a clue, hopeless! But you, you're a genius, you'll walk it, a doddle!' And I went to sleep reassured, contented that my dearest of friends was still alive to me.

In this extraordinary book you'll read Bernie's story in his own words, spoken to his new friend Charmaine Carter at a time when he was growing too weak to organize and write down the words himself. On every page you will hear the authentic voice of the author, a brave man who believed to the very end that he could beat the thing that was trying to kill him.

Matching his courage, Siggi and their son Ray watched over Bernie's final year while keeping up a magnificent lie. They both knew that Bernie could not survive – the doctors had told them that from the very start – but they managed to keep the fact secret from him. You don't tell a man who's going into battle that he's not going to win. If you have enough love to bear it, you stay in his corner and cheer him on to the very end. That's what Siggi and Ray did, at God knows what emotional cost.

But for me and so many others, Bernie Winters cannot be gone. He's in the next room or on tour or in Spain or anywhere except right here at the moment. Physically absent, that's all.

I know what they say but, like John O'Hara wrote, I don't have to believe it if I don't want to.

Bob Monkhouse, 1991

1

EARLY WINTERS

BERNIE WEINSTEIN made his debut on 6 September 1932 weighing in at a massive fourteen pounds. Apparently the nurses at the Salvation Army Maternity Home in Islington, north London, immediately nicknamed me 'Primo' in honour of the then heavyweight boxing champion of the world, Primo Carnera. It's still a matter of wonder to me how I was so huge. My mother, Rachel, was a tiny woman of Romanian Jewish stock; her father had come to England to escape the pogroms. My father, Samuel, was of Russian Jewish descent and just five feet seven, though just as broad. I was the youngest of three. I had a sister, Sylvia, who was six when I was born and a brother, Mike, who was three. I made my presence felt, though. I was the loudest and toughest and couldn't be ignored; the Bam Bam of North London.

Rachel and Samuel, who was also called 'Mougie', Russian for naughty boy, both came from large families themselves and we had numerous aunts and uncles who played a large role in our childhood. Mougie was one of five sons of Michael Weinstein, all of whom were characters in their own right. Grandfather Weinstein ran a restaurant in Parfatt Street in London's East End and was renowned for his strength and bravery. Legend has it that he alone stood up to a threatened attack by some violent anti-Semites who entertained themselves by ransacking homes and businesses belonging to Jews.

Most people hid when they heard of the impending attack, but Michael made it known that he was fully prepared to defend to the death both himself and his restaurant, and the attack was called off. Physically he was no weakling; apparently he saved a woman from certain death when she was run over by a tram by lifting it off her single-handedly. Mougie certainly inherited his strength.

Mougie's brothers, Shimmer and Harry, both emigrated while still young, Shimmer to New York and Harry to Australia. We completely lost track of Harry, who changed his surname to Winston, but we discovered afterwards he had become a Justice of the Peace. I met Shimmer years later when I went to America and was amazed to discover how like Mougie he was. Despite his age he took me to numerous nightclubs and really showed me some of New York's high life.

Our other two uncles, Benny and Mitchell, stayed in London. The latter earned his living as a bodyguard and was so effective that he was generally referred to as 'Mad Mitchell'. Benny often worked with Mougie and a couple of Rachel's brothers trying to make their living by gambling – mainly by running books at racecourses. They weren't exactly an established name; it was more like setting up with a small cash flow at the beginning of a meeting and having to run away if they lost the first race – frequently a lot faster than the horses they'd backed. One of my earliest memories is of hearing the brothers fight when they lost, each of them trying to blame another one for miscalculating the betting.

Mougie too worked as a bodyguard. He may only have been short, but he was very strong and wasn't afraid to fight. At one stage he looked after Major Jack Cappell, a sporting impresario, who had a few over-enthusiastic competitors. One of them hired an American gangster type to settle a few scores, Mougie included. He jumped Mougie as he strolled down Shaftesbury Avenue minding his own business and shot him in the leg. This annoyed Mougie somewhat, who responded by knocking a few of his teeth down his throat. If the fellow hadn't managed to escape, he'd have been minus a lot more than just his teeth.

Dad didn't like racist abuse, either, and was always ready to fight it. It was irrelevant how many he'd have to take on or how big they were. There was an enormous slob on a bus one day, at least six foot three, but when he started to spout anti-Jewish slander Mougie got up and punched him. He fell backwards and whimpered as he left the bus at the next stop. Mougie made sure that he taught Mike and me how to defend ourselves, and I took advantage of this by forever sending my older brother into battle on my behalf against any of the kids at school who were nasty to me. Mike wasn't too happy about that, but at least he won.

Rachel was very much the centre of our family. It was she who kept good food on the table and kept us and our home spick and span even when Mougie was going through a losing streak. She was very calm and philosophical and didn't moan when her prized possession, her diamond and platinum ring, went into the pawn shop yet again. I do remember, however, her going absolutely berserk when Mougie cashed in her faithfully invested insurance policy. This carried all her dreams with it: when it matured she was going to buy her own home – something she'd always wanted. When Dad put the whole lot on a horse that never made it to the finishing post, she hit the roof. Mougie didn't forget that in a hurry. Mum often sought solace in fortune tellers and believed them completely when they told her good news. She once came home in a state of excitement with the prophecy that Mike and I would one day be rich and live in a castle. I told her that when that happened I'd buy her bracelets to go all the way up her arms. She was always very hopeful for all of us – sure that Sylvia with her lovely singing voice would be another Sophie Tucker and that we boys would make it on the stage. She always told us, 'Aim for the stars and at least you'll get out of the gutter.'

Not that we lived in the gutter, but life for the Weinsteins in the early 1930s was hard. There was very high unemployment and Jewish people, like most foreigners, were barred from many jobs. It was a question of doing what you could to make a living, and even then not a very good one. It was normal procedure in our neighbourhood to have luxuries like fruit on the table one day and then be going round to the pawn shop with basic possessions like bed sheets the next. Pawnbroking was one of the few thriving businesses. We didn't starve but Rachel, like most other mothers, hoped her children would grow up to a better life.

She was one of seven children and her father, Jack Bloomfield, supported them by running market stalls selling clothes. In fact he started the now famous Chapel Street market in Islington. The boys he spawned, however, didn't follow in his footsteps. Micky, Connie and latterly Abe tried alongside Mougie and Benny to scrape a living by gambling and bookmaking. Joe and Jack became very successful boxers. Joe twice fought for the British Middleweight Championship and Jack, known as Gentleman Jack, twice took the British and Empire Light Heavyweight Championship. Later on they ran a pub in Leicester Square called the Champ's, and Mike and I were to meet a lot of show business personalities there. Luckily, although I admired my boxing uncles greatly and they provided me with a lifelong interest in the sport, I never succumbed to the temptation of trying to follow in their footsteps. So all in all Sylvia, Mike and I had an interesting heritage, but fortunately show business steered us away from the careers we could have had as fighters or gamblers.

Performing came entirely naturally to all of us kids. Sylvia sang, Mike did impressions, and I started off by doing impressions of Mike's impressions before discovering some of my own. Mum and Dad took us nearly every week to the Finsbury Park Empire to see variety shows, and I fell in love with the comics. I'd come home and burlesque whoever I'd seen, trying to duplicate their costumes and props. If it was Sid Fields I'd put on Mougie's coat and trilby, draw a little moustache on my face and try to mimic one of his characters, Slasher Green. I also tried Jimmy James, Claud Dampier and Mortimer Snerd, the dummy worked by Edgar Bergen, who had buck teeth. Way back then I fell in love with the idea of making people laugh, and it's something that's never left me.

When I was still quite young, about five I think, the family moved from the Islington flat to a house in Tottenham. I got the blame for the move; it was supposedly because I made a lot of noise banging my tricycle against the walls and the complaints from the downstairs neighbours forced us to leave. In Tottenham Mike made friends with a boy called Georgie Marks who lived over the road, and the three of us would mount little shows in our garden where we'd do impressions and sing songs. We actually managed to get other neighbours to pay to come and see us. Those shows were my first professional bookings and after that there was no turning back, even though I felt like it many times. Winning a talent competition while on holiday in Canvey Island when I was seven sealed my fate. I gave them my best impressions of Claud Dampier and Lionel Barrymore and won a shilling. Not only was it a wonderful feeling making people laugh, but you could get paid for it – what a fantastic way to make a living!

As well as giving me my first taste of show business Mike also got me into the odd scrape. One day he'd incurred Mum's wrath by playing swords in the living room and breaking a few prized ornaments. He decided to run away from home and unfortunately took me with him. We went to the recreation ground on the River Lea. It was fun at first. We had taken some food with us and had a huge picnic, but as it got darker I got more scared. Mike was, too, and it was just as we were sneaking back in the direction of home, hoping our absence hadn't been noticed, that we were hauled into the air by our huge uncles Micky, Abe and Jack. I don't know what was more petrifying, our angry uncles or the thought of spending the night out in the dark. They decided to teach us a lesson and hung us by our feet over the river. I remember crying, and luckily it was Mike who felt the brunt of Mum's anger and worry when we got home. Needless to say, I didn't spend much time by the river after that.

Unfortunately I had to go to school. I wasn't keen on that at all and, other than to get my brother into fights against other schoolkids, there didn't seem much point: unlike Mike, I wasn't a natural academic. I did meet Lionel Blair's sister, though. His father, Myer, had a barber's shop near us where I used to get my hair cut, and Lionel went to the same school and synagogue in Crowland Road as Mike and I. Lionel introduced me to my first sexual encounter at the tender age of seven: cuddling on the couch with his sister and dancing partner Joyce. It must have been a good start, because as I got older I definitely got more interested in the subject. It wasn't long, though, before the war intervened and I was parted from my first love.

At first the family stayed in London. Mougie determinedly built a shelter at the bottom of the garden, which he furnished for maximum comfort with cushions and electric light. He wasn't going to let the Germans get us, oh no. Mum wasn't impressed, however, and in her normal, philosophical way decided that if there was a bomb out there with her name on it, she'd rather it got her in her own home. As usual she won, and we didn't bother with the shelter again. Before long the bombing increased and we went, with the rest of the street, to the local Roman Catholic church for shelter. Our Uncle Joe, one of Rachel's brothers, was with us on one occasion when some roughs yelled at us: 'Watch the Jews run!' It didn't take them long to regret it after Mougie and Joe had finished with them.

Soon Mike and I were evacuated along with thousands of other London kids. We were sent first to Potham in Wiltshire to live with a lovely couple who looked after us royally, but unfortunately that only lasted a week; then we were moved to another house in Trowbridge. The people there were very nice but we just didn't get enough to eat, so by the time Mum and Dad came down to visit us we were starving hungry. Mum took us away immediately.

Back in London the bombing had increased and Anderson shelters and Roman Catholic churches no longer offered enough protection, so it was down into the underground stations. For us kids, most of what happened during the war was fun. We didn't understand the implications of what was going on or the dangers, so moving around the country, spending nights in Manor House tube with hundreds of other people and generally managing to avoid school were hugely enjoyable. Even when a bomb hit Holborn underground, killing everybody sheltering there, we didn't really understand the significance. Shortly afterwards Mum moved us again, this time to a suite at the Regent Palace Hotel. Mougie had got a job running a gambling club in Soho and was doing quite well. I liked living in a hotel, but it didn't last long because part of it was bombed and Mum hauled us off again, this time to join our Aunt Lil in Cowley in Oxford.

It was in Oxford that I realized I wasn't going to be a great scholar. While Mike was passing every entrance exam going, I was busily moving from school to school and hating them all. I went to a total of five in Oxford and, before the war ended, another three in London. I was deeply unhappy, always being picked on either for being a Cockney or for being Jewish, depending on whether I was in the country or in London. People in Cowley had a peculiar attitude towards Jews: one lady said we couldn't be Jewish because we didn't have horns growing out of our heads, while someone else said it was impossible because we didn't wear all the robes. It was like being from another planet, and I didn't like it.

Luckily we had a lot of our family down there with us; as well as Mum's sister Lil there was her husband Phil and their son Mervyn, whom I teamed up with so I could ignore the locals and their funny attitudes. Mougie got a job at the Morris factory where Phil worked, but he wasn't cut out to be an employee and, after a couple of disagreements, they parted company. Mougie then moved back to London. Uncle Phil stayed on and, in order to keep Mervyn and me out of trouble – we'd recently been threatened with shotguns by a local farmer when we'd burnt down one of his haystacks – he'd take us with him when he went out collecting the wreckage from crashed planes. Mervyn and I saved the German crosses he gave us. He couldn't watch over us all the time, though, and we'd sneak away to try and lie our way into local dances. We were twelve by then and very impressed with the RAF and American boys we saw there. Unfortunately one of the Yanks wasn't so impressed by my trying to chat up his girlfriend, and punched me on the chin. I ended up crying in the corner; so much for trying to pretend that I was sixteen. Sylvia, being eighteen and very pretty, used to bring a lot of RAF boys home and Mervyn and I would sit in the room with them, gazing in wonder at the personification of our heroes until we got slung out with a Hershey bar each. It was after some of them went off on a bombing mission one night and never came back that the full horror of war hit us and we finally realized what it meant.

Fortunately Cowley was not a common air raid target, but some nights we could see London burning from there. Mum was trying to earn some money at the time by selling ladies' underwear at the local market. She'd frequently travel to London for supplies and it was on those nights, as we waited for her to come home unscathed, that the London flames suddenly seemed perilously close. It was a very frightening time, and I found that I only felt safe when I had my Uncle Micky's boots with me. Micky was one of Mum's brothers and my favourite uncle. Later on he was very instrumental in Mike's and my career, but then he was my hero. He was an army sergeant and whenever he was with us on leave I'd stagger around in his enormous boots, keeping them tucked under my bed at night for protection. When he was finally demobbed he let me have them, and for years I wore them whenever Mike and I were on stage.

While we were in Oxford, Mike and I began to get interested in music. He was given a clarinet for his fourteenth birthday and, as I'd always enjoyed bashing things and making a noise, I was given a set of drums. The neighbours weren't overjoyed about our new pastime but we became really keen players. At the time Mike was constantly reminding me that I was an educational jerk. He was at the City of Oxford School, one of the best there, and was destined for the university. He'd picked up an incredibly snobby accent and was forever trying to correct my Cockney – not very successfully. When he was sixteen he took the Oxford University entrance exam and nearly passed. He was due to try again a few months later, but in the meantime he'd got the clarinet bug and instead went to the Royal Academy of Music in London.

Other than when Mike and I practised our music, I hardly saw him and was left kicking around in Oxford. One day I saw a poster for a show called *Watch on the Rhine*, which was on at the New Theatre in Oxford – and lo and behold, my old school chum Lionel Blair was in it. I travelled into Oxford to surprise him that night and asked for him at the stage door. He finally came out with the air of an artiste who is being disturbed, sighed, told me that he was really far too busy to see me and went back in. I couldn't believe it – he had all the airs and graces of a seasoned performer and enough make-up on to sink a battleship. Over the years Mike and I have worked a lot with Lionel and he's still one of my closest friends, but if ever he gets uppity I remind him about that night at the New Theatre.

It wasn't long before Mum brought me back to London and I started at another school in Tottenham. I hadn't exactly forgotten that I was Jewish, but several dozen of the boys took it on themselves to remind me by laying into me and really beating me up. Every day it would be the same, with one or more of them giving me a good hiding. Eventually I came up against the toughest boy in the school and luckily managed to stand my ground, so everyone avoided me after that.

I did have some friends, though; Johnny Rubens was one of them, and he was about as keen on school as I was. Between us we managed to contrive ways to miss out on most lessons. In the morning we'd be sent off to collect all the pupils' war savings stamps. We had to go to Stamford Hill for those, which was a few miles away, so we managed to while away most of the morning doing that, getting back just in time for the lunch break. Afternoons were generally spent collecting milk bottles and painstakingly placing each of them neatly in their crates. That was about the extent of my education, and at the grand age of twelve I decided to give it up as a bad job.

Life was much better after that. I started up on my own little business selling condoms at dance halls; my sales pitch was 'Buy me and stop one' and it seemed to work – I did very well. In between sales I'd get on the drums to practise my craft. I decided that I wanted to be either a world-famous drummer or a gangster. My great friend was Danny Sewell, younger brother of the actor, George Sewell. He'd been taught to box as soon as he could walk and had also finished school – he'd been forced to leave, though, after punching a teacher. We dressed like gangsters with stetsons and smooth suits; it makes me cringe now to think of how we must have looked, but at the time we thought we were the bees' knees. We had friends with names like Tony the Limp and Fat Sid; with Danny around we got quite a reputation for being hard nuts, so other heavies left us alone. By this time Mike could hardly understand me any more. I talked in the tough Cockney lingo of the time, whereas he'd become quite plummy, but he was fascinated by all the villainy and would sometimes come out with us to the Lyceum Ballroom to have a look at gangsterland. He wasn't quite so pleased when I returned the favour and went to visit him, though. The hallowed halls of the Royal Academy weren't the same after the gang had invaded, with their swearing and slang and generally oafish attitude. Mike was absolutely appalled and forbade me ever to cross the threshold again.

He did let me go to the Stage Door Canteen, however. That was set up in Piccadilly during the war to entertain the troops, and some of the biggest names in show business performed there for no pay. I frequently found myself in the same room as stars like Bing Crosby and Bob Hope, Paulette Goddard, Tony Hancock, Jack Warner, Googie Withers and Anna Neagle. It was incredible just to see people like that in the flesh, and if I didn't already have stars in my eyes I definitely developed them then. Mike was there as part of the entertainment: the Royal Academy had been asked to provide a quartet to play there, and Mike, with his clarinet, was one of them. They did very well and shortly afterwards the manager, a Mr Thackeray, asked Mike if he'd like to form his own three-piece outfit and provide an act that was more than just music. Fortunately he'd forgiven me for embarrassing him at the Academy by then and invited me to play drums in the trio. We set to it and rehearsed songs, dances and a comedy routine, using our well-tried impressions of my old pal Mortimer Snerd, Ronald Colman, Lionel Barrymore and Charles Boyer. Mougie used to sit with us for hours on end while we practised our act, willing us on enthusiastically.

At first we did a simple music routine, but then one night we broke into the act we'd rehearsed so hard. We danced and joked and sang and, astonishingly, the audience loved it. What an introduction to show business. Unfortunately it was going to be a long time before we got another reception like that. The soldiers who cheered us that night were wonderfully kind and friendly – they appreciated anybody who played at the Stage Door Canteen. When we went out on the road and came up against a paying public things were very different, but the encouragement we had from that start kept us going for years. Had we been older we might have given up when times looked bad, but we were teenagers and we knew we'd succeed.

Our act started with a song 'We are here to entertain you. We are here to stop you feeling blue . . .' and that was to be heard over the next few months in the strangest audition places. We must have seen or tried to see every single agent in London and we'd show them our talent any time or anywhere – we weren't proud, just eager. We played the toilets in Charing Cross Road for one, as well as numerous corridors; once we even auditioned in the street. Uncle Micky of the big boots came into his own at this point as well. Whenever he was on leave he'd take us around to meet his friends, who were mainly club owners, and talk them into giving us a chance. That way we managed to play places like the Blue Lagoon in Carnaby Street. That was an incredible place. We met the young Tommy Cooper there, who became a good friend of mine in later years, but the club itself was a real rough house packed with hoods and hoodlums – the bouncers on the door were employed to remove their shooters on the way in. Uncle Micky did well by us, though: he managed to get us included on the bill when entertainment nights were set up for his own Royal Artillery unit in Rowley and Aldeburgh in Suffolk. We were playing to good audiences but so far not a penny had passed into our hands.

Then I got my first paid job. Uncle Connie, another of Mum's brothers, was involved with the Regency Club in Soho; I was given ten bob to go along and play my ukelele, tell a few jokes and sing. I wasn't brilliant, but at least I wasn't laughed off stage. Mike and I were still enthusiastic about our double act, even though we couldn't find an agent daft enough to sign us up. Instead we earned a few shillings here and there playing at weddings and bar mitzvahs and appeared – for nothing, of course – at the Nuffield Centre, another wartime entertainment hall for the troops in London. It was worth doing, though, because there were always agents there on the lookout for new talent. It was at that time that we met another comedian who would one day be famous – Eric Morecambe. Still performing solo at the time, he wore a funny suit which was too tight for him, white socks, a string bow tie and black boots and sang a song that went: 'I'm not all there, there's something missing. . . .' Maybe he meant Ernie! He too would later become a good friend. We also did a charity show at the Victoria Palace Theatre in London and, even though we weren't marvellous by any means, the impresario Jack Hylton was apparently heard to comment that one day Mike and I would make it to the top. It was hearing things like that that kept us going.

By the time my own bar mitzvah arrived Mike was seventeen and due to join the merchant navy as a catering boy, while Mougie had got a job with some bookmakers in Blackpool; so it was to be bye-bye London, Mike and showbiz for a while. We had a wonderful celebration for my coming-of-age ceremony, with lots of lovely food laid on by Mum, and all our aunts, uncles and cousins came to join us. Then we left for Blackpool. What we didn't realize then, though, was that Mike actually suffered with sinusitis. Well, suffer's the wrong word. He never had a day's discomfort from it, but a merchant navy doctor diagnosed it before he ever got to sea. He was put on sick leave and eventually discharged after six months, without having done a single day's duty. I, in the meantime, was having a whale of a time in Blackpool. I got myself a job working one of the rides on the Golden Mile funfair and spent every night at the dance halls. I lost my virginity up there under one of the piers, and fell hook, line and sinker in love with a young Italian girl who lived in Scotland. I was convinced this was it and tried to save up enough money to run away with her, but if she'd waited long enough for me to earn even the fare to Glasgow I think we'd both still be there.

After six months Mougie's job was coming to an end and we were all about to return to London when I heard about a talent contest in Manchester, so I got in touch with Mike and we entered our double act. Luckily for Mike we won, and it led to a tour of Yarmouth and Lowestoft. It was lucky for Mike because, having been deemed unfit for the army, because of his sinusitis he was about to be drafted into the coalmines as a Bevin Boy.

That tour turned out to be a fantastic break for the both of us. On it was a pianist who was about to start a job running a Canadian Army Show Unit which was part of the Canadian Legion, and he asked us if we wanted to join him. Did we want to join? We couldn't believe our luck. So there we were on the road for the Canadian war effort.

2

THE WINTERS' WAR EFFORT

Our time with the Canadian Legion was wonderful – we never wanted it to end. The pianist was called Sammy Kearns and he really took us under his wing, teaching us the basics of performing – timing, what to do with your hands on stage, how to walk and, the worst bit, how to slap someone. He seemed to enjoy practising that on me quite a lot. We played to some really appreciative Canadian servicemen as well, including colonels and generals, and we were often asked back to the officers' mess. On one occasion there were three VCs in the room; we were really rubbing shoulders with the heroes and top brass. Fortunately they liked us a lot, and so our act got better and better.

We adapted easily to the Canadian way of life, especially as we were paid rather well and got good expenses. We were based at an enormous house in Farnborough in Hampshire, travelled about in big army trucks and wore uniforms that were a mixture of Canadian and American army gear. After a while we could fall into talking with Canadian accents at the drop of a hat; we found this a bonus when chatting up girls, who at that time much preferred Americans to English boys. We came a cropper a couple of times, unfortunately: the most embarrassing was when we were flashing our Canadian Legion badges at a couple of girls at the Lyceum in London and some old pals, realizing what we were up to, shouted: 'You're not still trying to get away with that phoney Canadian accent stuff!' Whoops. Mike had a worse one, though. He got very friendly with a girl who worked in the record business and she fell for the Canadian act. All was fine while they went out together, but then she cropped up time after time and Mike found himself still having to put on the accent for years afterwards. We were very busy as well, though, travelling from camp to camp every day and then performing at night. After a while Sammy dropped out and Mike took charge, with an acting captain's rank. Very impressive. I didn't rise through the ranks, however; I stayed an entertainer.

After a while we met a fellow who was doing the same job for the American equivalent of the Canadian army show unit. He was called Joe Baker and spoke with an American accent, and for a long while none of us twigged that any of us was English. Eventually he told us that he was the cousin of the film actor Bonar Colleano. Well, we knew that wasn't true because we'd got to know Bonar quite well during our Stage Door Canteen days and he often joined us in our army shows, so we were intrigued by this Walter Mitty character. It never occurred to us that he was probably equally intrigued by us with our fake Canadian accents, until one night after we'd all drunk too much he eventually leaned over and asked us if we were really Candian. I admitted that we were Londoners, then challenged him. 'I'm a Londoner as well, from Streatham,' he replied. We've been friends ever since.

By the time we were demobbed we were very confident about our act and sure that there would be agents queueing round the block to sign us up, particularly as all the guys on our unit had told us that we would be bound for success if we went back to Canada with them. Oh, how naïve. We did manage to find an agent, but sadly he hadn't learnt the art of finding work for his artists. For a while we were trapped as we were under contract to him, so in order to keep us alive I went to work in a warehouse – something of a comedown after the life of Riley in the Legion. Luckily the 'Buy me and stop one' business was still alive and kicking as well, but the shortage of bookings wasn't doing Mike and me any good and we were worried about getting rusty. Eventually, after a bit of heavy stuff involving Mougie – who basically told our agent that if he didn't release us he'd tear him limb from limb – we were on our own again. We did get some work but they were very poor bookings, and we'd find ourselves playing to near-empty houses. Then our luck seemed to turn.

Our Uncle Micky was friendly with a well-known Jewish agent called Johnny Riscoe; he told Riscoe all about his two star-struck nephews and pestered him into giving us an audition. At the time our act, if you can call it that, involved a musical satire which featured Mike on the clarinet and me on the drums. Our comedy material was pretty threadbare, and I was still playing the straight man while Mike delivered the gags. Although we knew that Johnny had agreed to see us only to get Uncle Micky off his back, he did give us a fair crack of the whip and we subjected him to our full repertoire – such as it was.

Johnny seemed particularly impressed with Mike's clarinet playing, and at the end of our audition we were amazed and delighted when he offered to book us into a new touring show which was due to open at the Palace Theatre, Walthamstow. We were even more staggered by the news that we were to be paid a joint fee of £15 a week – less Johnny's commission.

The show itself starred a well-known comic of the day, Hal Blue. Johnny came up with the idea of using Mike's clarinet playing to open the show with a rendition of Gershwin's 'Rhapsody in Blue' – and in fact he decided to call the show *Rhapsody with Blue*. At that time I was billed as 'Burn', a nickname I had been given by the boys in the Canadian Legion. We were very excited. Okay, we were nowhere near the top of the bill, but playing to London audiences again was a big chance for us.

All our confidence came back with a surge, so much so that I was too cocky to rehearse. Very silly mistake. When we got on stage that first night I completely dried. I couldn't remember a word, and my tongue stuck to the roof of my mouth. Not so the rest of me – that was soaking. I perspired enough to fill a bath. The plan was that we'd start off with our new signature tune which was 'Sing, sing, sing . . .', then Mike would say 'Good evening, ladies and gentlemen' and I'd follow with 'Good evening and it's nice to be back in England after two days in Tooting.' I'm word-perfect now, but that night I could not remember a thing. Nothing – I couldn't even make a vague stab at it. I just stared at the audience with my mouth hanging open. Mike tried his 'Good evening, ladies and gentlemen' three times, desperately trying to prompt me, and then after the fourth I managed 'Hello, Mike.' Needless to say Mike was absolutely furious and was going to stop me doing the second house, but our friend Joe Baker, who was there selling ice creams – much more lucrative than performing – refused to go on with him, so he was stuck with me. Unfortunately the humiliation of forgetting everything hadn't had the desired effect and I spent the whole week only remembering half the sketches. We even tried switching roles, but it didn't work. I simply had a mental block, and nothing I did would shift it.

Not to be discouraged, we stayed with the show. It toured for three months playing at various 'number two' theatres. The best thing for me to come out of that tour was the experience of working with a great comic such as Hal Blue. He possessed masterly timing and superb mannerisms, and I know that I learned an awful lot from him.

Amazingly enough, despite our distinct lack of success, Johnny still managed to find us more work. He approached a well-known entertainer called Len Young, who was known as 'The Singing Fool'. Len used to produce his own variety shows and was about to stage a new revue at the Metropolitan

Theatre in the Edgware Road, a very famous old musical theatre. Johnny heard that Len was short of one comedy spot and convinced him that we were just the boys he needed. He landed us the job and our money went up to £25 a week. Unfortunately, once the show opened Len let it be known that he found our act about as 'funny as a funeral', and he told Johnny he would never book us again.

Twenty years later, when Mike and I were top of the bill enjoying a record-breaking summer season in Blackpool, Johnny Riscoe paid us a visit backstage in our dressing room. Although he was no longer our agent, we had always remained on good terms. I will always remember what he told us that night. 'Boys,' he said, 'I hear you're each earning a four-figure fee for doing some bloody act that Len Young hated all those years ago – I knew I should have charged him more than £25 a week!'

Not surprisingly, the work didn't exactly come flooding in after that episode. In fact we did nothing at all for quite a while. How Mum and Mougie kept their faith in us I'll never know, but Mum was convinced we'd make it. 'One day you boys will shake a Pagoda tree' she'd say, sure that we'd be successful despite all the evidence to the contrary. Mougie was sure as well – so much so that he carried on supplementing our income, even when we were performing, so that we could afford to do it. After a while we managed to get a bit of work again. It was cabaret in a nightclub in Oxford Street, and the wages included a flat over the club. What we didn't realize till we moved in was that we were sharing it with a couple of prostitutes, and all the to-ings and fro-ings of their clients kept us awake all night. For an innocent like me it was quite an eye-opener!

By now I was sixteen and had just a few months before I was due to be called up. There didn't seem to be any point in joining the army any more as the war was over, so I planned to join the merchant navy if I could. There was just enough time to take a couple more bookings before that, though, including one in Ireland, and we certainly made the most of it. Dublin was an incredible city. We'd never been there before and of course they'd had no rationing, so there was wonderful food to be eaten, booze to be drunk and clothes to be bought on the cheap. The Theatre Royal was paying us £40 a week which seemed like a fortune, and we certainly lived it up. We were billed as Americans, as the Irish weren't keen on English comedy at the time, and we went down exceedingly well. It was the high life that kept us there, though. After our fortnight's booking was over we decided to hang around to see if we could get more work. I was enjoying myself tremendously and Mike was dating Miss Ireland, so neither of us particularly wanted to come home. But our money ran out pretty quickly despite another week's work, and eventually we had to write home to ask Mougie if he'd help us. A wonderful girl named Blossom, who was an usherette at the Royal, took us into her home and looked after us until Mougie's money arrived. When it did we thought we would spend some of it on a thank-you gesture to Blossom for her kindness. We planned to hire a car and drive into the country for lunch. But we'd forgotten one thing – none of us could drive. Mike had a go first and nearly drove straight into a lamp-post. Then it was my turn. For some reason the car always seemed to lurch forward when I was trying to brake, and after nearly killing a few innocent bystanders we decided to give up and throw a party instead.

Eventually we came back to London and joined a revival of *Rhapsody with Blue*. But after the first performance we regretted the decision – we were going down like a lead balloon. It was so peculiar; the Irish had loved us, and here we were falling flat on our faces in our home town. It all came to a dreadful end one night when the magician who preceded us ran off stage halfway through his act. We were shoved on in an attempt to cover up his thoroughly obvious and sudden absence, and in the process Mike fell over my drums. Like a recurring nightmare I felt the familiar dryness in my mouth and the sweat starting to pour. I'd gone again. When Mike finally dragged me off stage, after a dreadful few minutes which seemed like an eternity, we were sacked. To add insult to injury, as well as booting us out the theatre manager spat at us, saying, 'Get out of the business, you're useless.'

I started to wonder whether we'd ever make it in show business and got very depressed as I tried to wheedle my way into the merchant navy. It had become very competitive since Mike's day, and it was important now to show that you had a craft to offer. I applied for a position as a waiter and took along a bundle of references from local restaurants. I'd never waited on a table in my life, but they obligingly gave me glowing write-ups and I got the job. My first post was as a silver service waiter on a Union Castle ship about to sail around Africa, and unfortunately, unlike Mike, I passed the medical. When I realized that this was a top-class ship and that the passengers probably had silver service every day of their lives I started to get worried. Then when they handed me an enormous platter laden with huge fishes I was as nervous as on any bad night in the theatre. The dining room was the longest room I'd ever seen, and it was so sedate with its chandeliers and soft music that I felt clumsy before I even began my long walk – or stagger, more like – to the other end. The idea was that I should lift the fish expertly on to the individual plates, then move elegantly on to the next diner. It didn't quite work out that way, though. I managed to get the spoon underneath the first fish but, rather than being lifted gently, it flicked up into the air and shot across the table, straight into the horrifyingly expensive lap of a lady diner. In the meantime the rest of the fishes slid unceremoniously on to the floor by my feet. I was allowed one more go, but when I dropped a whole stack of plates I was demoted. If we hadn't already been on the high seas I might well have been thrown off the ship, but they managed to refrain from doing that. Instead I was reduced to the soul-destroying task of scrubbing the cooking pots.

The ship was very luxurious, but of course we were supposed to stay away from the passengers. That's all very well, but when the ladies are as beautiful as some of them on that trip it's easier said than done. I got a crush on one who was only aboard till we docked in South Africa, and she seemed quite flattered. Eventually I plucked up enough courage to speak to her, and then we arranged to meet on deck at the front of the ship at dead of night. I had to sneak all the way along the ship from our quarters at the rear without being spotted, and was relieved when I made it. She was, too, and we sat and talked together until the early hours. We were just about to kiss when torchlight rudely interrupted us. It was the master of arms and he'd found me out. So much for shipboard romance. After that I had to satisfy myself with playing poker with my mates and drinking. I won cases of cigarettes that way, but it was a lousy alternative.

I only ever got one other trip, and that proved to be a very different experience from the glamour and glitz of the first. This time we were carrying people who were emigrating to Australia, and the standard of the ship was dreadful – disease was rife and there was a large number of deaths. At least I had some friends with me. Half a dozen mates had wanted to join the merchant navy to avoid the draft and I helped them in – I was pleased to have their company as most of the other seamen seemed to be gay, and sometimes there's safety in numbers. I'd finally got over the humiliation of Mike's and my last stage appearance and was happy to entertain my pals in the evenings with my ukelele. We'd sing and drink and enjoy the evenings up on deck, and in return they'd let me have a couple of hours' extra kip in the morning.

I got stung a couple of times, though, but that was by passengers. I fell for the oldest trick in the book. Before we set sail, a Jewish family came up to me and promised me a good tip if I made sure they were always well supplied with food. They'd heard that the portions would be small aboard ship, and knew they could rely on a good Jewish boy to help them. As I was assistant steward on the voyage I could guarantee that I'd see they were all right. So what happened? They didn't turn up for the last couple of meals on the ship, which I thought was odd for a family so concerned with eating well. The next time I saw them was when they were shuffling guiltily down the gang plank, trying to avoid tipping me. Never again, I thought, but of course when someone else asked me for special treatment I took him on trust. When he pressed a measly two shillings in my hand, I gave it back. In fact you can really get to dislike passengers. Another one was giving one of my mates a hard time, and I offered to help him out. It was spaghetti day, so I carried out a huge plate of Bolognese and made my way towards the offending diner. Unfortunately a few paces away I suddenly tripped over my own feet – one of the stage tricks I'd learnt – and the slimy wet pasta landed in his lap. He didn't make a murmur for the rest of the trip.

I really wanted to see Sydney but normally wouldn't have been able to get shore leave, so I enlisted the help of one of Mougie's old bosses, Major Jack Cappell, the sporting impresario whose activities had got Mougie shot in the leg and who was now based there. He contacted the ship's captain and invented a story about how he was involved in top secret arms trading negotiations with the Australians on behalf of HM Government and could do with my assistance. For some obscure reason the captain fell for it. In fact not only did he believe the story, he gave me and several of my pals the whole week off. The Major's generosity didn't stop there, either. He provided a car for us and gave me some money. It's always useful to have family contacts.

I got in touch with another one while I was there, too. An old racing pal of Mougie's, the comedian Bud Flanagan, had a son called Buddy who had gone to Australia to seek his fortune and was now a disc jockey on a Sydney radio station. When I called him he was very welcoming, and invited me to the station to do an interview about working on board ship and being a comedian. It was all very friendly, and afterwards he told me about a talent contest that was due to be held locally that week. I entered and won, and for the first time since being bawled offstage back in London I thought that maybe I could make it in show business again.

That was my last trip for the merchant navy. I expect they were pleased to see the back of me. But now what to do on Civvy Street? Mike was otherwise engaged by then, running his own successful market trading set-up, so if I wanted to continue with my bid for stardom it would have to be as a solo act.

3

DUCKING AND DIVING

ONCE out of the merchant navy, in the early fifites, I developed my own act and tried to hawk it around London agents – but although I managed to get a lot of auditions, I fell flat on my face at every one of them. The idea was that I would sing 'Come Back to Sorrento', a quasi-operatic number, fall over in the middle and then be dragged off stage by my feet. Reappearing with my ukulele, I'd break into a rendition of 'Dusty Shoes', with dozens of shoes dropping on to my head from above the stage. It wasn't a bad act, but somewhere along the line I had lost the art of being a stand-up comedian. In fact I couldn't stand up at all. I'd contracted another version of stage fright – that of trying to perform whilst bent double. I looked like I was permanently taking a bow even before the act started. It was hard to convince an agent that they could have a potential star on their hands if they signed me up, when I couldn't even look them in the eyes.

I don't know how I managed it, but I actually got some work: first with a tour of a nude show – the pay was only £8 a week but that was all I could afford! Then I performed closer to home, at the Collins Music Hall in Islington. I tried especially hard that night because Mum had come to see me, but a drunken heckler started to have a go at me and I got so upset that I couldn't get through my act. Eventually I begged him to give me a chance as I was a local boy and my Mum was in the audience.

He left me alone then, but the damage was already done and I gave up performing for a while.

There didn't seem much for me to do other than to follow Mike into the family business of market trading, and my brother was happy to sponsor me. While I had been in the merchant navy Mike and a friend of his called Ray Stott had built up quite a business selling women's stockings at street markets all around the country. You couldn't exactly describe their merchandise as top of the range: 'the family' had put them in contact with suppliers of somewhat imperfect goods. They would buy thousands of imperfect and unmatched silk stockings of varying colours and sizes, then spend hours attempting to pair them off and package them neatly to look like the real thing. Some didn't have any heels, and often the match wasn't exact. But they certainly sold – mainly because of the sales spiel Mike and Ray had managed to learn from the top traders around the country. If things went wrong – say they had sold the wrong size to someone – an irate husband would turn up the next week looking to make trouble. Mike developed a very convincing army history to cope with that one. 'Of course I didn't sell her the wrong size intentionally,' he'd say to someone ready to punch him. 'Do you think I enjoy standing here in all weathers? I don't have any choice. It's because of the malaria I caught when I was serving out in the Far East.' There'd be tears after a speech like that, and other women around the stall would start shelling out in sympathy. Mike and Ray learned pretty early on not to return to the same market too quickly, and by the time I joined the business they were doing so well that they were employing a small army of traders to go around the country on their behalf.

At least what I had learnt on the stage was at last being put to good use. I was so good at the sales patter I could have sold a pork sausage at a bar mitzvah. In fact on my first outing I got the record for selling all my stock in the shortest time ever. The only problem was that I had let my partner for the day well and truly con me. The idea was that I gave the spiel and got all the customers interested while this chap took the money. I was very worried about him during the day because he told me he was a diabetic, and the poor bloke had to keep going off to the toilet. What I didn't realize was that each time he disappeared he put half the takings in an envelope and posted it to his home address, so that by the time I triumphantly returned to Mike's office with a wad of money it was in fact 50 per cent light. Mike hit the roof, and after that I had to buy my own stock. On one trip out I found myself flogging so-called *haute couture* stockings with no feet.

Mike had to bale me out of trouble a few times though. I'd been selling stockings hand over fist at Rochester market when a wealthy-looking lady came back for seconds. I thought I had hit the jackpot, but instead she produced a Board of Trade inspector's card and I was nicked. Mike said that whatever I did I was to plead guilty in court and then not say a word. But when the magistrate said, 'Do you not realize this is an imprisonable offence?' I gasped and feebly stammered, 'But my brother said it would only be a £5 fine.' Luckily I got off with a £25 fine.

It wasn't such a bad time. After all, who could complain about being chased by a load of women – even if all they wanted was the missing feet to their stockings. But my frustrated quest for stardom could no longer be suppressed, and whether or not there was any money in it I just had to get back on the boards.

I'd met up with my old pal Joe Baker again. In the meantime he had been playing some of the worst dives and was getting nowhere, so he turned his hand to working on the other side of the fence as an agent in Greek Street. There then followed a period of total confusion: one day he'd be the agent booking me into jobs and the next I'd be doing the same for him. At other times we'd both end up as agents and occasionally as a double act. But at least we were getting work. I was still nervous about being on stage and couldn't stop standing there like a hunchback, but Joe would come with me for moral support. It meant that when I was at the Bury Hippodrome in Lancashire we spent my fee and his commission on keeping us both up there for the week. At least I did well there: the audience gave me a good reception, laughing in all the right places, and I felt as though I was on the up again. Unfortunately it was short-lived. The audience at my next booking in Halifax stared at me in complete silence, and I was back to being an agent again.

I didn't know what was worse: falling flat on my face on stage for a measly £15 per week, or booking third-rate acts into third-rate venues for seven shillings commission. My mind was made up for me by a theatre manager called Paul Rogers, who wanted to book a comic for a week in Dewsbury, Yorkshire, for £8. I decided to become my own agent, and ended up staying with the show for three weeks. We went on to Newcastle, Grantham, then Grimsby. Why Paul Rogers kept me on I'll never know. I was a disaster from start to finish, and by the time we got to Grimsby I was so badly heckled that I couldn't take it any more. I wanted to run away, but instead lied my way out of having to face the Grimsby audience again by saying I had got my call-up papers.

How I did it I don't know, but I took another booking shortly afterwards in a show at the Swindon Empire. I wasn't doing too badly, but obviously was not impressing two Americans sitting at the front who kept passing rude comments about me and chucking cigarette butts on to the stage. In the end I had had enough. I leaped off the stage and punched one of them in the face. That certainly shut both of them up, and the rest of the audience loved it.

Mike had been very kind to me during my attempts to go solo. He would travel round the country to support me in different shows, and even offered an agent money to put on a show built around my act. But unfortunately the agent had a reputation to protect and would not be bought in this way. Mike was going from strength to strength in his clothing business: he had moved on from dodgy stockings to set up a mail-order clothing business out of an office just over the road in Greek Street from Joe and me, and we took advantage of being on his doorstep by creating a tabletop soccer game and staging our own matches between the top teams of the time. It was like an adaptation of Tiddlywinks. The counters were players which were flicked across the pitch toward cardboard box goals at either end. These matches became the high point of the day and attracted large audiences of people like Spike Milligan and Harry Stevens, who were supposed to be working in the same office block.

Unfortunately, whilst attendances at the game got better and better Mike's business got worse and worse. His stock had been stolen several times, to the point where he couldn't get insurance cover. Then his last-ditch attempt at survival turned into a damp squib as well. He had managed to lay his hands on one of the first deliveries of big-collar button-down shirts to be imported into Britain, and was offering them with an initialled tiepin thrown in. The orders flooded in, and Mike was delighted to be back in business. Then disaster struck. The factory where the tiepins were due to be made burned down and Mike was forced to buy them elsewhere, but as the price suddenly went up by ten shillings for each tiepin Mike was out of pocket by five shillings on every order. Up till then business had just been doing badly, but now he found himself facing huge debts. There was little for it other than to try and resurrect our double act.

I was staying at Mike's flat in town at the time, and as I got ready one night to go down to Chatham naval base for a booking he suddenly asked if he could come too. Not having been incredibly successful on my own, I was delighted to have him along. We decided on the way down that we'd carry on as before, with him as the funny man and me as the sidekick, but as Mike walked on to the stage and the sailors started to whistle at him he lost his nerve and told me to be the funny man. We went down brilliantly that night and decided we would really try to make it work this time. However, as usual the rest of the world was not yet ready for us and we had a hard time getting bookings. Luckily Uncle Micky was only too pleased to try to get us work again, and it was almost like *déjà vu*: auditions in streets and toilets for anyone who'd spare us ten minutes to watch our act.

Uncle Micky's world was night-time Soho and he knew most of the club owners there. He managed to persuade his friends to let us perform at Churchill's, the Panama Club, Murray's and the Stork Club. We really thought we'd made it by the time we played the Stork Club, as one of Uncle Micky's friends had promised to get Bernard Delfont to come and see us. Our act was magical that night, with cheering and encores from the audience. We knew that Mr Delfont was bound to be impressed, and he might well have been had he actually been there. Eventually two weeks later one of his deputies did come to see us and, despite our hopeful faces, told us straight that we didn't stand a snowball's chance in hell of becoming stars. To say that we were deflated is an understatement, but somehow something made us carry on and it wasn't long before we got our first real break.

We had been playing the Hollywood Club in Soho when Uncle Micky bumped into Jack Farr, one of his old racing pals. Jack had been a musical comedy dancer in a successful act called the Three Loose Screws until war intervened. Now he was trying to start up the act again and needed two additional performers. Although we could not claim to be anywhere near as experienced as Jack's other co-performers, he agreed to come and see our act. We were over the moon when he signed us up. Six weeks later, after frantic rehearsals and having acquired a dog called Lulu, we played our first date in Aldershot. At last we had a real job.

4

LOVE, ROMANCE AND A BIG SUIT

W^E would stay as two-thirds of the Three Loose Screws for two years, although it would be unfair not to include Lulu as a big part of our act and our life. In fact she stayed with Mike and me for six years in all and was probably responsible for starting my love for working with animals which still goes on to this day, with my huge St Bernard Schnorbitz. Lulu had nothing of the pedigree of her successor – she was a scruffy mongrel. But she had a heart of gold and acted her part to perfection. Her first role was in a sketch where Jack sang a song about trees and held his arms out like branches. Then the inevitable would happen. Lulu would come on stage supposedly looking for somewhere to cock her leg, and when she spotted Jack in his tree pose he'd run off.

Off stage Lulu was our responsibility, and anywhere that we stayed while on tour Lulu would stay too. This caused a few problems at first, because she wasn't house-trained or used to the dark. Whenever we turned the light off to go to sleep she'd start to charge around the room like a wild animal. Mike and I would end up standing on the bed clutching each other and trying to keep away from her gnashing fangs. Eventually she calmed down and became the sweetest pet and artiste in the business, but she had a strange way of showing her affection for other female stars. The Three Loose Screws tour took us to the Hippodrome in Brighton, where the singer Anne Shelton was top of the bill. During a break in rehearsals Anne left her sheet music lying on the stage. Lulu made a beeline straight for it and proceeded to pee all over it. I was terribly embarrassed and apologised profusely – not very convincing while Lulu was running around wagging her tail and obviously enjoying every second.

In all other respects she behaved like a true professional, even to the extent of reserving her best performances for the fullest 'houses'. When business was bad she would come out on to the stage and slope across with her head and tail down. When it was good she'd perk up, holding her head high and with her tail going around like a high-speed propeller. She was such a clever dog that we could leave her in the dressing room at the beginning of our act and she would come out on to the stage on cue, do her piece and then go straight back to the dressing room unescorted.

It wasn't long before I was completely besotted with her and we became inseparable. She slept with me at night on my bed, ate with us – she wouldn't touch dog food – and went everywhere with me, never more than six inches away from my heels. She was a good guard dog too. When we were on tour with Tommy Steele and hordes of his fans were threatening to engulf us she snarled so viciously that they suddenly fell away and made a path for us. Another time we found her barking at some policemen who were trying to move our car. She could look really wild when she was angry, and they didn't dare go anywhere near her.

Lulu never liked me having girlfriends, feeling that she was being upstaged. She would treat them like they didn't exist. When I met my future wife, Lulu seemed to sense that this was more serious and purposely turned her back on her, making a big show of ignoring her. It was only years later, when my wife became pregnant, that Lulu finally forgave her and began to dote on her as well. She'd had her own puppies by then and knew what motherhood was all about.

But back to the Three Loose Screws. The act was always building and improving, until by the second year we were booked for the whole season in Weymouth. For Mike and me this was the point in our career when we felt we could claim we had become professionals. Jack was a marvellous comic and teacher and we learned an enormous amount from him, including how to dance. Later on Mike and I were renowned in the business for having the best finish to our act, a complicated tap routine involving knee drops, and it was all down to Jack. Unfortunately he was also an ardent gambler, and even though from my childhood I'd vowed never to get involved in such a mug's game I found myself falling in with Jack's conviction that he had discovered the perfect betting system. Several hundred pounds later I realized I was wrong and so was Jack.

This was not the ideal introduction to a young German girl I had just met and fallen in love with, especially when I lost her money as well. Her name was Siggi Heine and she was a dancer in the show during the season at Weymouth. It was 1955 and I was twenty-three by now, and up until then I'd only ever had casual relationships with the girls I had met. But right from the beginning I knew that Siggi was different.

I first set eyes on her during rehearsals. She was part of the chorus and I'd been told by a friend of mine to look out for her as he thought she would be my type. He was absolutely right, and I found myself turning into a stammering jelly when I first tried to talk to her. I finally plucked up enough courage to invite her to lunch at the caravan that Mike and I had rented for the summer. She was not like any other dancer I had met, insisting she would only come if Mike's girlfriend Cassie was also there. I spent hours preparing lunch that day, and by the time we had eaten I thought I could tell that she liked me. Mike and Cassie tactfully left us alone and I sat down next to Siggi to put my arms around her. Big mistake! She was absolutely furious. I was so taken aback that I escaped into the kitchen and frantically started to clear up, but I was so upset that I grabbed hold of a pan that was still boiling hot and burned my hands. Within seconds Siggi turned back from a snarling tiger into a purring pussycat – she fussed over me then and for days afterwards. I had embarked on the rockiest romance of my life.

I did not impress her either when I offered to give her a lift back to London from Weymouth at the end of the season. Mike and I had an ancient Hillman Minx at the time and the car was packed with people, all contributing towards the cost of the petrol. Unfortunately it did not even make it up the hill just outside Weymouth, so I had to ask two of the people to get out. Later on it broke down, and while I was desperately trying to fix it I tore a huge hole in the seat of my pants. By the time I got Siggi home to east London it was seven o'clock in the morning, and her stepfather came to the door like a volcano. I already knew that he didn't like me very much, and this certainly wasn't helping. First he tore me off a strip for keeping Siggi out all night, and then when I turned round to leave and he saw the hole in my pants he just roared. I ran. I was convinced he would persuade her not to see me again, and that she wouldn't need much persuading. So I was amazed when she later agreed to come out with me again.

The end of that season down at Weymouth marked the end of Mike and me and the Three Loose Screws. At first I thought it was a real shame, as we'd done so well with Jack. We weren't top of the bill, but we were near it; we'd gained incredible experience and we'd even made our first television appearance – on a Saturday variety show for the BBC. It seemed to me to be a terrible mistake to break up the act, but unfortunately there had been a disagreement about money. Right since the beginning the deal had been that our pay was to be split among the three of us on a 50–50 basis – half to Jack and half to us. As Mike and I were playing a larger and larger part in the act, we asked for the split to be made three ways, but Jack wouldn't agree to this. So we felt that we had to go our own way, and we had a lot of encouragement from other 'pros' to do so.

I still don't know if it was the right decision. We got work as a double act in a few shows, performing with Benny Hill, George Formby and Max Miller. Max was a lovely man and tried very hard to help us, but it wasn't long before our work ran out completely. Then we had another difficult decision to make. Should we take work in Europe entertaining American troops, or carry on trying our luck in England? The rumble in our bellies made up our minds for us and we left for Germany. But a full stomach was no substitute for an empty heart. I found myself missing Siggi more than I could ever have imagined.

Our European tour didn't exactly start off with a bang. While we performed our socks off, hundreds of huge and hostile GIs would simply stare at us to the point where we thought they might get violent. We realized pretty quickly that we had to adapt our act to meet their taste, and reverted to the way we'd performed in our Canadian Legion days. Amazingly, they fell for our Canadian accents, and all of a sudden they started to like us – so much so that one night one of them came over and accused us of pretending to be Canadian when we were obviously from New York!

The longer I was out in Germany the more I grew to hate it. We did three shows a night, and even though we were very popular we often found ourselves playing to a bunch of brawling drunks. Sometimes I nearly feared for my life when things got really out of control. It was like being in a war zone. There were nights when we didn't even bother to go on and the audience was so drunk they didn't even notice.

Other nights we wished we hadn't. There was very strong racism in the US forces to the point where blacks and whites sat on separate sides of the hall and all we could do was pray that nothing would spark them off. One night a black GI ran up on to the stage and started dancing to the music. We were convinced that a race riot was about to ensue. Not knowing what better to do we just carried on playing until he'd had enough. Luckily we'd done the right thing. In Würzburg the men were in such a violent mood that in order to keep them quiet the sergeant ordered a load of guns to be pointed at them.

When we first got to Frankfurt I really did think it was the end. It was midwinter by then and the snow was falling so thick and fast that when we got into our car after the performance we could hardly see a thing. Mike was at the wheel and drove straight into a parked car. Honourable as usual, he left his name and address for the owner of the wreck. The next morning we were patting ourselves on the back about our honesty when in trooped several armed policemen. Our hearts sank to our boots as they asked for Mike and escorted him away to the police station. He told me later that he'd been really shaken when one of the top brass at the station appeared complete with metal hook in place of his right hand. Mike was envisaging all kinds of dreadful things, when suddenly the fellow grinned and told him how delighted he was to meet him as he'd had such a wonderful time in England when he was there as a prisoner of war.

All in all the GIs were a pretty frightening bunch but at least we expected them to have proper security, so we couldn't believe what happened when we were at the air base at Nancy in France. On the night we actually performed there it took us a few hours to get in, what with all the identity checks and searches. But a few days later, when we realized we'd forgotten some of our props, we returned to find absolutely nothing in the way of security. Everyone had gone off to Paris for the weekend and the whole German army could have walked in unchecked.

After a month I was desperate to see Siggi again and Mike was really missing his girlfriend Cassie. We took to long, hard nights of poker to try and win enough money for the fares home. For the first fortnight we looked in danger of losing our shirts to various GIs but then our luck turned and one night we won

£750, more than enough to get us back to London.

I had a wonderful week with Siggi, and Mike didn't do so badly with Cassie – in fact they decided to get married that week. The stag night ensured that I didn't remember much about the wedding day, but Mike was the happiest I'd ever known him. The only fly in the ointment was that Mum refused to come because Cassie, like Siggi, wasn't Jewish.

I was delighted for Mike, of course, but because we went back to Stuttgart with Cassie, but without Siggi, I felt more lonely than ever. In fact I became a real gooseberry and wouldn't leave the newlyweds alone. I'd keep them up at night playing endless games of Scrabble when I'm sure they had much more interesting things on their minds. Then Siggi really took me by surprise – she came out to Germany without telling me. But it wasn't quite the romantic encounter she'd planned. The hotel clerk gave her the wrong room number, and she went absolutely berserk when she opened the door to find a couple in bed together. She ranted and raved for a full five minutes before she realized that I wasn't one of them. When she did find me I was so happy to see her, and so delighted that she had wanted to come all the way to Stuttgart to see me, that I spent my last fiver on an emerald engagement ring and asked her to marry me.

To my delight she accepted, and as we walked around the town that night with our arms about each other we started to talk about the future. Another big mistake! I'd naturally assumed that our children would be Jewish, even though Siggi was not of the faith. She obviously hadn't assumed any such thing, and our wonderful evening of tenderness and romance came to an abrupt halt as we yelled at each other in the street. Finally she tore the ring off her finger and threw it on to the ground, screaming that she did not want to marry me. We both watched in horror as the ring slowly rolled down a drain. Engagement number one lasted all of half an hour. I didn't know then that there'd be another two – plus rings – before we finally married, so I was heartbroken when Siggi left to come back to England.

After that I didn't see her again for a few months. Mike and I finished our European tour after visits to Paris and Rome, and I was relieved to get back to England. Although the Americans liked us I hadn't enjoyed it at all, but coming back to England proved to be a bit of a disappointment. Not only did Siggi not want to know me – neither did any agents. It certainly wasn't 'Absence makes the heart grow fonder' in either case. We had been away long enough for people in the business really to ignore us. It took a while for Mike and me to realize that it was time to overhaul our act completely. We'd been so busy adjusting our accents and language to suit an American audience that back in England we were like foreigners. We scraped some work in Portsmouth and Birmingham, and died a short and horrible death at both of them.

At least in Birmingham I met Siggi again. She was dancing with the Keith Beckett Trio and was booked on the same bill as us at the Hippodrome. We took great pains to avoid each other up until the opening night when we could not help but meet. When I actually saw her I realized how much I'd missed her and asked her out again. Before long I'd bought engagement ring number two, which cost me £25 and had real diamonds in it. That one lasted a lot longer: a whole three months.

Despite our dreadful failure on stage Mike and I were booked for a whole summer season at the Palace Theatre in Blackpool. We tried our hardest: after all, you can only take so much failure. But though we may have deserved top marks for effort we hit zero as far as our performance was concerned. Strangely enough, the guys running the show wouldn't let us change anything in our act. We couldn't understand this, because we were supposed to be comics and never raised a single titter. We discovered later that they were having big laughs with their mates at our expense, watching us fight for our lives every night. I must admit I was having a good time off stage. There were friends down there, lots of parties and lots of women. So many women, in fact, that the ceiling below the bedroom in the house we'd rented gave way at one point. Enter Siggi, followed shortly by the wrath of the whole German nation. I tried to talk my way out of it, but realized I was not succeeding as engagement ring number two flew out of the window.

So the Blackpool season ended with a whimper for me, both professionally and personally. As I busily licked my wounds Mike hauled me off to Dublin for another booking. Surely this one would work – after all, the Irish had loved us before, hadn't they? Their memories were obviously shorter than ours, and by the end of the first week Mike and I seriously began to contemplate jacking in the whole thing.

Then came the turning point. We'd thrashed ideas around for a fully forty-eight hours, knowing that it was make or break time and searching for just one small flash of inspiration that might save us. Even when we hit on it we didn't know it. Mike suggested that we should try dressing me up in a huge baggy suit. Up until then we had always been immaculately turned out on stage in evening dress. We'd done it out of respect for our audience, but in fact we'd dropped a clanger. There was nothing visually funny about us – we looked like a couple of MCs rather than a comedy double act. We found a tailor willing to construct the sloppy, baggy mess of a suit and decided to try it out on stage the night it was ready. So incredibly nervous were we that, unusually for us, we had a drink before the show. Thus fortified, we went on. I staggered across the stage a couple of times, looking about me as though I did not know where I was. The audience loved it, and as a nervous reaction I emitted one of my 'eeeh's' – that went down well too. After that we could do no wrong, and got more laughs that night than in our whole career up to that point. It was unbelievable. After being in the depths of gloom we were suddenly on the road to success.

Sadly, I was still Siggi-less. When we got back to London I went to see her grandmother – about the only member of the family left speaking to me. She told fortunes by cards, and even though I'd found it hard to believe her she always said that Siggi and I would get married. I constantly phoned Siggi, and her house must have looked like a florist's with the amount of flowers I sent her, but to no avail. As far as Siggi was concerned I was history.

Mike and I got some work, though, in Sunderland with a chap called Tommy Steele. While we had been in Dublin Tommy had become an overnight superstar with his first hit record, 'Rock with the Caveman'. We had never heard of him, and thought that the pimply youth we were introduced to must be a porter or something. Instead it was the star himself, and what a great guy he turned out to be. He had become so successful that the two weeks' tour ended up lasting a year, and it was really good fun.

Tommy was a real practical joker. I've lost count of the numbers of hotels we were thrown out of because he'd order smelly fish on room service for unsuspecting guests and would remove shoes and laundry left outside doors. One night he pulled a fast one on his manager, Johnny Kennedy – we'd had an impromptu party in Tommy's suite with some local nurses, by the end of which Johnny was legless. We helped him into the shower to sober him up a bit, but he crawled out, so Tommy decided to put him to bed. Bed was a mattress in the hotel lift, and we waited until one of the guests used it. It was lovely to watch an innocently snoring Johnny disappear behind the lift doors and then, when it was called to the next floor, hear the surprise as the lift doors opened in front of some guests. In absolute bewilderment Johnny woke up and told them to get out of his room.

Then Tommy had a go at me. We were down in Dover and he asked me if he could borrow my car for a quick trip to London. Two days later he was back minus my car. 'I'm sorry,' he said, 'I left it too late to drive back, but your car is safe in Gerrard Street. If you go and collect it tomorrow I'll pay your train fare. I promise.' Like a mug I went up to Soho, but could not find the car anywhere. I had to rush back to Dover for the show that night, and when I told Tommy it had disappeared he threw his eyes up to heaven. 'I'm such an idiot!' he said. 'It's not in Gerrard Street at all. It's in Denmark Street.' I refrained from hitting him, and returned to Soho the next day on another useless mission. The car wasn't in Denmark Street either. The penny still hadn't dropped when the next day I went back to Soho, this time to pick the car up from Long Acre. Guess what? It wasn't there, and this time I wasn't going to refrain from hitting him. I got back to Dover, fist at the ready, but Tommy managed to talk himself out of getting whacked and told me my car was twenty yards down the road in a car park. Amazingly we are still friends.

When our tour reached London Mike and I saw our names in lights for the first time. All we could do was stand and stare – it was such a momentous occasion. The night before our debut we went out to celebrate with our cousin Mervyn and Mike's ex-business partner Ray Stott. We chose Olivelli's, a favourite restaurant for showbiz people. But I nearly choked when we walked in to find Siggi having dinner with a new boyfriend. I could not stop myself from going over to her table. She was equally astounded at seeing me, particularly when her date asked me to leave and I told him in no uncertain terms what he could do with himself. He didn't like being spoken to like that, and within minutes we were fighting out in the street. It turned into a battle when two of his friends appeared and joined in, while Mike and Mervyn came to my defence. There were fists and knees and blood flying everywhere. We crashed through the restaurant windows and hurled each other against parked cars. Siggi came out to shout abuse at me, and then the police arrived to stop us all. We managed to convince them that despite all the havoc it was just a minor disagreement, and we could not imagine how the windows had got broken. Luckily they did not press any charges. Mike had to have his forehead stitched, and two of the other guys who were acrobats suddenly found themselves enjoying an enforced holiday, one on a stick and the other with his arm in a sling. Siggi vowed never to speak to me again. You can imagine how we looked for our West End debut. Not exactly a night for Mum to be proud of us.

She changed her mind, though, when shortly afterwards we appeared at our local Finsbury Park Empire and were invited along with Tommy Steele to take part in a new TV programme for teenagers called *6.5 Special*. Mum even went out and bought a new television to celebrate. But she wasn't too impressed and told us in no uncertain terms that we were 'all right': not brilliant, just all right. Be that as it may, we were booked for a year. At last we felt like real stars and people would stop us in the street and ask for our autographs. It was wonderful!

All during that time I still tried to persuade Siggi to come back to me, but she was adamant. Eventually Mike and I made a record called 'How Do You Do?' I sent her a copy, then telephoned her, and incredibly she spoke to me. Mike and I were in pantomime in Glasgow at the time, but were due to come back to London to perform the song on the Jack Jackson TV show that weekend. She agreed to meet me and over champagne at the Stork Club I produced engagement ring number three – a beautiful opal which had cost me £40 – and popped the question. Fortunately she accepted, and we were married three weeks later. If she'd held out any longer I'd be up to the Koh-i-Noor by now.

We were married on 28 February 1958 at Caxton Hall in Westminster. I wore the blue suit I'd had tailor-made in Glasgow, and Mum and I travelled together to the Registry Office. On the way she noticed I had matched my beautiful suit with a pair of old brown boots. 'What on earth are you wearing those for!' she exclaimed. I didn't want to admit I couldn't afford new shoes, but she insisted on stopping and buying me a new pair. It was just as well, as there was a crowd of press photographers waiting for us. Siggi and I had a lovely reception at the Grosvenor Hotel in Victoria, which I am still paying for, but we had to wait ten years for our honeymoon.

5

Do You Want to Be a Star?

IKE and I thought we'd really made it after our success on *6.5 Special* – so much so that we invested in our own touring show. We played venues as far afield as Brighton, Glasgow and Liverpool and outnumbered the audience in nearly all of them. It was peculiar. We'd done so well before that we didn't think we could lose – how wrong we were. It appeared that nobody wanted to know us without Tommy Steele or *6.5 Special*. So when producer Cubby Broccoli asked me to appear in one of his movies, how could I refuse?

By then Mike and I were in pantomime in Southsea, but dreams of becoming a movie star encouraged me to take the job. The film was called *Idle on Parade* and starred Anthony Newley and William Bendix. It was a comedy about national service life and Tony and I were to play characters with the same name whose army records got mixed up. Movie work was completely new to me and I was thrilled by it all. In fact I was so enthusiastic that I kept introducing new lines and ideas for my character, just as I would do on stage. Incredibly, instead of throwing me off the set they encouraged me to improvise, and my booking stretched from one day to four. It obviously went down well with the producers, because in the final film my part was much larger and Cubby Broccoli offered to sign me up on a five-year contract. If only it had been ten years later I might have ended up as James Bond!

The offer put me into a terrible dilemma; to do it I'd have to give up the double act with Mike. At the same time the possibility of making it in the movies was irresistible. There followed a great deal of soul-searching and late-night discussions with Mike, most of which were very tense and unhappy. I felt dreadful letting him down, particularly as it would mean cancelling a lucrative summer season in Great Yarmouth, and I knew that Mike's financial commitments were about to grow as he and Cassie were expecting their first child. Eventually we agreed to break up, on condition that we kept to our normal arrangement of splitting our earnings. I know that the idea of taking half my movie pay for nothing embarrassed Mike enormously, but it was the only way I could forgive myself for leaving him in the lurch. What I didn't realize at the time, despite my five-year, £100,000 contract, was that my actual pay was hardly going to be worth dividing.

Jazzboat was the first movie, and for that I earned £750 over six weeks. Mike and I ended up with about £30 a week each. There were three others after that: *In the Nick*, *Let's Get Married* and *Johnnie Nobody* – each of them as bad as the others. They paid me £1000, £1500 and £2000. Quite where the other £95,000 was supposed to come from I don't know.

Although none of the movies was particularly good, I thought I didn't do too badly in the first two. *Johnnie Nobody* was a complete embarrassment, though. There was no comedy in it at all, and my script included words like 'ecclesiastical'. I couldn't say it then and I can't say it now. We must have done more than thirty takes and I still couldn't manage to spit it out. When I saw the finished movie I was never more relieved that my part had been cut to a mere split second.

We filmed at Bray in Ireland, and my only solace was to drink myself into oblivion with Oliver Reed every night. He was working out there at the same time, starring in a Robin Hood film. We got ourselves into some incredible punch-ups after these late-night boozing sessions. Nothing really changes, does it?

Tony Newley and I became almost inseparable during my brief movie career. We'd known each other since we were teenagers and we'd meet at the Grand Café in Soho, a popular venue for up-and-coming young actors. Unfortunately, while he was becoming a movie star my own prospects were waning. He was also becoming a very successful singer and was starting to have hits. My cousin Lionel Bart, of *Oliver* fame, wrote one of them. It was called 'If I Say I Love You, Do You Mind?' and I sang an extra 'Do You Mind?' at the end of the song. The record went straight to number one, but unfortunately the record company chopped off my bit.

Despite all his amazing success, however, he wasn't much better off than me, and a couple of times we got together to do a double act in Royal Variety Club shows at the Savoy Hotel just so that we could grab a free meal. I don't know what was more embarrassing, the way we performed together or having to sing for our supper. Either way, we decided in the end to go hungry.

We were very good friends, but sometimes he would throw the odd wobbly. A few years later, when he and Joan Collins were on their honeymoon in Malta, we discovered that we were all staying at the same hotel. I knew Joan as well by then, and Tony was delighted to see me, so we arranged to have dinner. They were also shooting a film out there, combining business with pleasure, and one day when they returned to the hotel after work Tony waved out and said, 'See you in half an hour for dinner.' I sat and chatted in the bar with Frankie Howerd until he suggested that he and I eat together that night. When I explained that I was meeting up with Tony and Joan he said, 'Are you sure? Tony can be a bit funny sometimes.' Sure enough, when I rang up to the room to see if they were coming down to join me Joan said they couldn't make it. Needless to say, Frankie enjoyed saying, 'I told you so' later over our meal!

Siggi and I were living an almost schizophrenic existence at this time. We'd go to glossy film premieres, dressed in expensive clothes courtesy of the Cubby Broccoli bank account, and I'd be driven to movie studios in grand limousines. But all the time we were living in a two-up, two-down terraced house in east London with barely enough food on the table. I really wanted to make it in the movies, but after a year of earning practically nothing I realized that to get the money promised in my contract I'd have to make an awful lot more movies in a very short space of time. Eventually it clicked that it just wasn't going to happen. Before I made a final decision I asked the film company for a loan of £1500 so that I could buy a nicer house, closer to the studios in Boreham Wood. They let me have it, and when I later told them that I was leaving they told me that I now owed them £1500 – so I told them they still owed me £150,000, according to Cubby's new contract with me. We managed to reach a compromise: they could deduct the £1500 when they paid me the £150,000.

While I was busy playing at being a movie star Mike was busy trying an assortment of careers. I know that I was not very popular at the time, especially when his half of my income was so laughably low. First of all he tried to write a novel which he called *The Black Mass Murder*, but he wasn't too enthusiastic about the thought of becoming a novelist and so he took small parts in radio plays for a while. Eventually he moved into the show promotion business, starting a company called Winc Productions with Jack Murray, who'd put on a lot of rock 'n' roll shows. Mike wasn't as successful at this venture as he should have been, mainly due to bad timing. He put on shows with Englebert Humperdinck and Gary Glitter before they became famous. I guess he was the Martin Peters of show promoters – ten years ahead of his time. Some time later he proved it when Jack Murray offered him a part share in an up-and-coming pop group. Mike turned him down flat as he was busy with other things. Jack did, too, as he couldn't afford to go it alone. That group later became the Beatles.

Mike also tried his hand at producing a couple of plays. The first was *Lucky in Love*, but unfortunately it was only after he sold out to another producer it took off and became a money-spinner. The second was *The Little Hut*, which ran quite well but didn't bring Mike a fortune. I was going to invest in one of his ventures: a show with Bernard Bresslaw, the singer Mike Preston and Ronnie Corbett. However, business looked gloomy and Jack Murray and I had to pull out. But I'm delighted to say the show was a huge success for Mike. All in all I think he did a lot better with his show promoting than I did in the movies.

We did work together from time to time during that period. One occasion was a promotional show for my third film, *Let's Get Married*, at a cinema in the West End. Tony Newley was the star, and Mike and I performed our act too. It wasn't a brilliant booking, but it helped Mike and me to stay friends and eventually to start up the double act again.

And we still had our football. When we'd been doing *Babes in the Wood* in Southsea, just before my call to movie stardom came, we'd started a team called the TV All Stars XI. A lot of friends played with us – like Tony Newley, Pete Murray, Tommy Steele, Jess Conrad, Alfie Bass, Ronnie Corbett and Bernie Bresslaw. And our brother-in-law Leslie Wise was team manager. I'd always adored football but didn't really get much opportunity to play. Mike was more of a rugby fan, but got more enthusiastic as our team took off. We'd started it because I could hardly ever get a game with the existing Showbiz XI. I was only allowed to play if the game was way out of London and Arctic conditions were prevailing. All the big stars turned up for the London games, particularly if they were televised, so more often than not there was no room for the likes of a small star like me in the team.

Our first match was against a team of Johnson and Johnson employees. We were amazed and delighted when hundreds of people turned out to watch, and that encouraged us to arrange further matches. Subsequent games against the police and others were so well attended that we started to take our playing really seriously. We even trained at Arsenal's ground at Highbury, and before long were playing matches every week all around the country. It became an addiction to the point where we'd travel from one end of the country to the other and back again just to get in a game.

Eventually the inevitable happened – we were challenged to a match by the Showbiz XI. The whole thing got ridiculously out of hand and we trained so hard it felt as if our legs were going to fall off. We had one pro player on our team, Malcolm Allison, who of course went on to become one of the most colourful and charismatic managers of all time. The Showbiz XI had two, Billy Wright and Wally Barnes. Also turning out for them were Sean Connery and my old friend Des O'Connor.

When the two teams got out on to the pitch the atmosphere was just like that of an FA Cup Final. The odds were against us winning, but we shook them with our fitness in the first half. At half-time Malcolm Allison gave us a good pep talk which convinced us that we could actually pull off a shock result, and we went back out for the second half really determined to go for it. As a result an over-enthusiastic tackle from Mike on Showbiz player Ziggy Jackson unfortunately broke his leg. We grabbed the winning goal in the last minute, courtesy of Malcolm Allison. It was incredible – a never-to-be-repeated moment.

We played with the All Stars for eight years in all and loved every minute, even if we became really unpopular with various agents. They would stand on the sidelines cringing as their stars got knocked about on the pitch, dreading the sound of a bone breaking in case it put their client out of action. Some were forbidden to play with us but did anyway and would sneak off, having to invent ludicrous excuses if they got injured. Tommy Steele's foot took a hammering one week, and when he got to the theatre that night he ingeniously removed a light bulb on a staircase so that he could pretend he'd fallen downstairs in the dark. I had to adapt my pantomime costume rather rapidly one year after I took a knock on my ankle and it swelled up to ten times its normal size; I pretended I'd slipped on the pier on my way to the theatre. I had another peculiar injury which made my leg get stuck in a certain position. It would happen several times during a dance routine, and Mike would have to step in and crack it back again.

We raised a lot of money for charity with our football games, which was another very good reason for playing them. The tragic Aberfan Disaster, when a Welsh slag heap collapsed on top of a school, happened during this time and we were able to contribute to the fund. By the time the team disbanded in 1969 it had raised £150,000, which was mainly distributed amongst children's charities.

So despite the unhappiness between Mike and me about my abortive attempt in 1959 to make it big in the movies, football played a big part in keeping us together. The summer of 1960 saw us back together again for the season in Jersey with Frank Ifield, earning £100 a week each – a darn sight more than you could get being a film star! It was a lovely summer; Cassie and Siggi stayed there with us, and we played a lot of football for our showbiz team. We even managed to persuade Frank to play one day, but unfortunately during the game he broke his big toe and had to hobble on stage, to perform his entire act sitting on a stool.

6

THE BIG TIME

IT is impossible to pinpoint the day that it happened, but in the sixties Mike and I became stars. That is not to say we did not have the odd disaster or up and down here and there, but in general we were at last moving in the right direction: upwards.

In 1961 we were on stage at the Palladium in a variety show with Shirley Bassey. The chairman of Moss Empires, Leslie MacDonnell, came to see us after our first night to tell us how wonderful we'd been, but in our enthusiasm we'd stayed on stage three minutes more than our allocated time. He told us that if we did it again we would be out on our backsides. Ironically, Shirley had to cut her act short the following night as she had caught a throat infection, so Leslie had to ask us to come to the rescue and do an extra seven minutes! We went down so well that we were the talk of the town. Suddenly our act was very polished with good comedy routines and a dance number at the end which brought the house down. It was an amazing routine, which took three or four months to learn and another six to perfect and involved some stunning moves. We did a series of knee drops, where you jump up in the air and land on your knees – which eventually did my cartilages in – and twenty-four 'cobblers', the Russian kick that you do from a crouching position. Once we had done those right across the stage of the Palladium people couldn't help but cheer. Bookers said we had the best finish in the business and the top impresario, Richard Armitage, was so impressed that he sub-contracted us from our own agent, Joe Collins. It was almost as though having a year off from the business had done us good.

In October Siggi gave birth to our son, Ray. We named him in honour of my mother, Rachel, and for Siggi and me it was a very happy time. We had our new home and a healthy bouncing baby boy, and at last I was earning enough to pay the mortgage and feed us.

Richard Armitage did quite well on our behalf, getting us several bookings on the television programme *Sunday Night at the London Palladium* – which unfortunately did not go too well – and the next year a summer season at Weymouth with Matt Monro and the Springfields. Dusty Springfield, she of the big blonde hair and thick black eye make-up, was a lovely girl but had a peculiar way of winding down after a show. She and her brother would finish their set, go to their dressing room and hurl crockery at each other. She'd have to go to Woolworth's the next day to replenish the stock for that night's relaxation. It must have cost a fortune.

Over the next year we did a lot of television. ABC-TV had started a new summer resort variety series which starred acts from the summer seasons in various northern resorts. We appeared on it frequently, and on one occasion when there was a hold-up in the recording Mike and I got up on the stage and entertained the audience for half an hour with jokes and sketches. The producer, Philip Jones, was really impressed by this and tried to talk ABC into giving us our own series. It didn't work, however, probably because of our abysmal reception on *Sunday Night at the London Palladium*!

It was to get worse. We were honoured and delighted to be invited to take part in our first *Royal Variety Performance* back at the Palladium. The forecast and the betting were that we would stop the show that night. Instead we died. We did completely the wrong material, never having played to an audience of that quality. We were used to people who cheered as soon as I walked on with my funny suit and said, 'Hooray, we're here.' That night you could have heard a pin drop, and right from the beginning I was thrown.

The rest of our five-minute spot seemed to last forever and went downhill all the way, and if we hadn't had our dance routine to finish the act we'd still be stuck on that stage now, thirty years later, trying desperately to get off. Thank you, Jack Farr of Three Loose Screws fame for teaching us to dance. We crawled back to our dressing room in abject misery, and the Scottish singer Andy Stewart was so sorry for us that he gave us a bottle of Scotch to drown our sorrows.

We went over and over our act, wondering where we had gone wrong and getting drunker and gloomier by the second – completely forgetting that after the show we were due to be presented to the Queen! I don't know how I even managed to stand in line, but I do know that someone told me that the proper form of address was 'Ma'am'. Suddenly she was in front of me, and I wanted the ground to swallow me up when I heard myself calling her 'Mum'. I tried to correct myself, and made it worse by bowing and calling her 'Your worship'. Why I didn't just shut up I don't know, but the next minute I was inviting her to the pantomime we were in that Christmas. So much for my first brush with royalty.

I don't know if Her Majesty came to our pantomime either that year or the next, but if she did she was incognito. What I do know is that during our panto the following year a film called *The Cool Mikado*, featuring Mike and me, was released. Earlier in the year the director Michael Winner had invited us to take part in the movie; as they were filming at Pinewood and we were in summer season in Weybridge we thought we could fit it in. If only we hadn't. It was dreadful, and poor old Mike nearly ended up giving Michael Winner a right-hander. Our script was supposed to be funny, but it just didn't work. At one point Mike was to say, 'That's Mount Fujyami. Look over there, Bernie'; then I was to say, 'What Mount Pyjami?' Well, that's simply not funny, and we thought we could vaguely help it by changing it around to 'Look over there, Bernie, that's Mount Fujyami.' 'Mount Pyjami?' Okay, that's not brilliant either – but when Mike put the change to Winner he indicated that when he wanted our suggestions he'd ask for them.

Our role lasted another three days and I spent most of that time trying to keep Mike from punching the director. In return he preferred to address Mike through me, always telling me to tell him what to do. We knew we would not like the movie, but we had to go and see it when it was released. Frankie Vaughan, Jimmy Edwards and Dave King were in the same panto as us at the Palladium and we all saw the movie together. When Mike came on screen Frankie and Dave fell about with laughter and poor old Mike was so embarrassed he left the cinema. But with constant barracking from the rest of us, with things like 'Come on, let's finish this rehearsal quickly – I want to see *The Cool Mikado*', Mike started to laugh about it.

Pantomime that year was a lot of fun. We were in *Puss in Boots* and the very funny Jimmy Edwards was a delight to work with. He used to say, 'You don't need talent in this game. All you need is the stamina to keep going.' He echoed that on stage one day when the Queen of Hearts said to him philosophically, 'We're here today', and he retorted, 'I don't know about "We're here today" – we're here for another bloody fourteen weeks!' We roared off stage, but the manager was not amused and told him 'You can't say that because we are all here to make a living.'

Little did I know at that stage that the manager was supplementing his income by taking all the money out of the box office. I can tell this story because he was caught and ended up going to prison. The Palladium was doing incredible business at the time through advanced booking money for a series of concerts by Sammy Davis Jnr. I rather stupidly went gambling with him after the show one Friday night and lost all my money. Mike and I were earning £150 a week each at the time, which was a very good wage. The manager and I played chemin-de-fer, and even though right from childhood I've known it's stupid to gamble I still had a go. On the first deal of the cards I lost £50, so I said to Siggi, who looked after my wages, 'Give me another £50, and then another', and within three deals I had lost my whole week's earnings. Of course, he was all right – he'd just go back to the theatre, open the safe and take out some more.

Our career was going well, but we felt we might have gone as far as we could go in England and were thinking about trying Australia or America in 1963, when we were suddenly offered regular appearances on the Russ Conway television show and a three-year contract with Richard Armitage. We decided to stay, and that was when we really started to make it. Shortly afterwards Russ pulled out of his show as he was having problems with his nerves, but the producer, Philip Jones, who'd liked us so much on the summer variety shows, managed to persuade ABC to let us have the series in his place. We were over the moon. We had our own TV programme at last and it was called *Big Night Out*. We only wished that our mum had still been alive to see us.

Taping for the show was in Manchester on Sunday nights. The rest of the week we were in summer season with Arthur Askey in Southsea, so we'd fly up to the studios on Sunday mornings and back again after the recordings. It was a hectic schedule, what with learning scripts and rehearsing as well as fitting in our regular games of football – but it was great fun and the shows were marvellous to do. Arthur was fabulous as well, giving us hundreds of jokes to put into the TV show. I stayed friendly with him for years, and visited him in hospital when he developed a thrombosis in his leg and had to have it amputated. He was immensely courageous and somehow managed to keep his sense of humour. He told me that if the doctor gave him an artificial leg he'd be able to do pantomime the next year. Then, laughing uproariously, he showed me a pair of tap shoes which Dickie Henderson had brought for him.

Big Night Out was always in the Top Ten. It attracted top name guests as well, and I was very embarrassed one week when the Beatles were on because I had been burlesquing their song 'She Loves You, Yeah, Yeah, Yeah'. I hoped they had not seen it, but John Lennon very sweetly told me he thought I was very good and thanked me for plugging the record. We also had people like Dickie Valentine, David Nixon, my old friend Matt Monro, Russ Conway, Vera Lynn, Billy Dainty, Petula Clark, Diana Dors, and novelty acts like the ventriloquist Albert Saveen with his schoolgirl puppet Daisy May. The odd thing about Saveen was that on stage he also had a small Yorkshire terrier puppet which sat perfectly still throughout the act except for when his jaw would suddenly drop open and he'd growl 'Shut up.' Mike and I watched entranced as Saveen rehearsed. We couldn't fathom out how he was operating the dog's jaw when he didn't have his hand up its back. It wasn't until we actually recorded the show that we realized it was a real dog with a false bottom jaw fitted to its head!

Our old friend Lionel Blair worked on the show with us, creating some great new dance routines, and he had to get back to London at night as well. We'd all be as high as kites on leaving, and after additional drinks on the plane would end up landing in a somewhat drunken state.

One night Siggi had come to meet me at the airport and was furious when I fell out of the plane. We had a terrible row on the way back, and I got out of the car in Kensington vowing never to go home again. I decided to drown my sorrows and completely forgot that the next day Mike and I were due to open at the Palladium. I got there at 5.30 and we were due on stage at 6.15. I was a complete and utter mess, and Mike had been going crazy not knowing where I had got to. I was still drunk, of course: I tried to reassure him that everything would be all right, but it wasn't. Every gag fell flat on its face. The audience stared at us, wondering what on earth we were doing; I started to get really nervous, perspiring buckets. What a way to start an eight-week run. Fortunately it couldn't get worse, and by the time Tom Jones joined the show we were playing to packed houses.

Siggi and I managed to patch up our differences, though, which was just as well as she frequently appeared on *Big Night Out* as one of Lionel's regular dancers. The audience didn't know till the last show of the series that she was my wife, and just to complete the picture Philip Jones filmed our son Ray, who was all of two years old at the time, banging away at his toy piano while I sang 'Pretty Baby'.

At this stage *Big Night Out* was only seen in the north and the Midlands, as the weekend London service didn't show it. But the first series did so well that Rediffusion bought the second series to show in the London area during the week. That was a great relief to us, because it meant that we could record the show at Teddington in Middlesex and not have to fly up to Manchester every week.

To launch the new series we booked the Beatles. They were coming back from their huge American tour that very day and we deviously arranged to have them brought straight from the airport and down the Thames, to arrive at the back of the studios away from the millions of screaming fans outside the front. We did a little sketch with them, in which Mike and I were customs officers checking their baggage. Mike was stupefied when I okayed their cases without opening them up. 'But you don't know what's in them,' he said. 'Oh yes I do,' I replied. And all four of them opened up their cases and flung thousands of dollar bills into the air. The Beatles were filmed all day prior to the show, and viewers at home got sneak previews before the proper programme started that night.

They were really nice boys. Somehow stardom did not seem to have gone to their heads and you could really have fun with them. We had a running gag for *Big Night Out* which involved me getting blown up every week at the beginning of the show. This particular week Mike and I donned Beatle wigs and the six of us played an unknown pop group searching for a name. We went through the Insects, the Armadillos, the Tarantulas, the Mike Winters Sextet and even the Beatles, but no one liked any of those names – particularly not the Beatles. As John Lennon suddenly had a burst of inspiration – 'I know, we'll call ourselves Cilla Black' – I switched off the light and the room blew up.

Also on the show they sang five of their hits, 'Hey, Hey Mr Postman', 'All My Loving', 'I Wanna Be Your Man', 'I Wanna Hold Your Hand' and 'Till There Was You'. The last of these was Paul's solo number, and it was fun to watch them during rehearsals as the other three jeered Paul's efforts to perform on his own.

In between numbers we staged another sketch together in which the Beatles and I pulled a gag on Mike. One by one they went up to him with a card bearing a supposed request from the audience. The first one read: 'Please can Bernie sing "Twist and Shout"', then 'We want Bernie singing "All My Loving"'. Eventually a mystified Mike pulled back a screen to reveal me writing out all these request cards.

Thanks to the Beatles, that episode of *Big Night Out* was sold to America – the one and only time the Winters brothers were seen coast-to-coast in the USA. We became very friendly with the group and would go to places like the Revolution Club together, which was fine until what seemed like millions of marauding fans discovered where they were. George Harrison once asked me to go on holiday with him to the South of France, but I turned him down. After all, you go away to relax and not be chased by hordes of effusive admirers.

Big Night Out was great experience for us. As well as learning more and more about how to perform in front of cameras, we did a lot of our own stunts. But they didn't always go quite according to plan. In one sketch Mike and I were cowboys having a fight. Mike was supposed to hit me over the head with a prop bottle which would smash easily, but somehow the glass was thicker than it should have been and I ended up unconscious on the floor. Another time I was supposed to burst through a 'brick' wall made of polystyrene after an explosion offstage. The wall should have simply fallen to bits as I touched it, but it had been made in the wrong material and when I threw myself at it only half my body got through – and that half was covered in cuts and bruises. Then it happened to Mike as well. We were playing Bonnie and Clyde in a sketch – needless to say I was dressed up as Bonnie – and it involved us leaping on to a bed which would then spring backwards into the wall. We had special straps to hang on to whilst the bed went flying, but they snapped and we were thrown on to the ground some ten feet below. That time we both ended up unconscious.

Even in our next television series, *The Mike and Bernie Show*, we carried on doing our own stunts. You would have thought we'd have learnt by then. I had to ride a bicycle into the river in the middle of winter, and Mike had to dive in from a bridge some twenty feet high. Then there were the animals. Poor old Mike had to sit on a camel while playing the clarinet. He managed to fall off three times before getting to the end of the number.

Having got away with burlesquing the Beatles, I had to try Tiny Tim. He was a guest on the show and looked so peculiar with his long hair and baggy trousers that I couldn't resist it, and the next week I came on with a long-haired wig singing 'Tiptoe Through the Tulips' and mimicking his falsetto voice. It went down a storm, and people at our stage shows would always ask me to do it again.

Our summer season that year was in Blackpool, and conveniently we were asked to do another television series, called *Blackpool Night Out*, which was to be taped up there.

Sophie Tucker was booked to appear on one of those shows, and it was a very moving occasion for us. When we were kids she had always been Mum's favourite singer, and I still remember hearing Mum singing her songs. Sophie was delightful to us, and when we broke into our finale, 'Bye Bye Blackpool', Mike and I and most of the audience were in tears. It was so sad when she died just a few months later.

Our television success meant that the houses were consistently good for our stage show, and we found ourselves sharing the bill with a fellow called Jimmy Tarbuck. At first he was very quiet and polite, almost touching his forelock, and we thought he was going to be a real bore. Little did we know. One day we were in our dressing room, where a telephone had just been installed. When it rang I picked it up, to hear someone saying that they were from Blackpool telephone exchange and were testing the new line. I was asked to count up to ten. Then I was asked to recite 'Round the ragged rock the ragged rascal ran', which I did, and then I was asked to whistle down the phone. I did, but nothing happened. So I whistled again, but still nothing happened. I said, 'Was that all right?'

'Not bad,' came the answer, 'but I'll get you two ton of birdseed and you'll probably be a lot better.' So much for the quiet, polite performer we had first met.

Old Jimmy liked a drink as well, and fortunately Blackpool was buzzing with parties and promotional events where you could be guaranteed a few freebies. The *Daily Mirror* hired the Imperial Hotel for three days, and everyone appearing in the theatres in town was invited for drinks and a buffet. Jimmy went every day. One day he just managed to stagger back to the theatre in time for the matinee. His opening number was 'Strolling Down the Strand with a Banana in My Hand', and as he lurched on to the stage he just managed to utter 'Strolling' before collapsing flat on his back. He had to be dragged off stage, but the audience loved it.

The following year we were again asked to do *Blackpool*

Night Out, but unfortunately our summer season was in Great Yarmouth this time. The only way to do both shows was to fly up after our Saturday night performance. But this time we were not on a regular flight route as we had been for our previous London/Manchester journeys: this time we had to go by small taxi-plane from a little airstrip near Great Yarmouth. Because we were flying at night the airstrip was lit with a double row of cans containing lighted rags. It really was hazardous, and each week we would only just clear the trees at the end of the runway. The pilot would rev the engine as we passed over the Imperial Hotel to let Philip Jones know we were on our way – it gave him time to pour our drinks before we arrived. The flight back often wasn't much better. Even though it was daytime it was still difficult to find this remote runway. Mostly we'd have to try to spot where Siggi and Cassie, who had come to meet us, had parked our cars.

Even though we hadn't really noticed it, Mike and Bernie Winters were by now big stars. Our shows always topped the ratings, and unbelievably we were one of the biggest showbiz acts in Britain. So it seems strange to think that we earned just £200 for a TV show and £350 per week for a summer season. But that was because of a contract we had signed three years before which kept our wages artificially low. Fortunately that contract was about to come to an end, but at least we had a good time in our last underpaid summer season in Great Yarmouth. My old and great friend Matt Monro was with us, as was Tarbuck.

I got a call one day in the dressing room. 'Mr Winters,' the man said, 'my name is John Blackthorne and I am phoning you from Ormskirk. I would like to invite you both to our pub to knock down a pile of pennies. It is in aid of our preservation society and I would be very grateful if you could come.' Needless to say I didn't fancy going all the way to Ormskirk, but the chap went on, 'There is a £100 fee and the national press are due to cover the event.'

How could I refuse? 'We'd be delighted to come,' I said. 'What pub is it?'

'The Queen's Arms', he answered.

'Okay,' I said, 'and where is the Queen's Arms?'

'Around the King's arse,' came the reply. It was the phantom phone caller Tarby again.

Our Scarborough summer season in 1966 should have been a real high point. Financially it was. Our restrictive contract was over, so our fees suddenly shot up. We got £1400 a week, and we asked for our first pay to be in cash so that we could finger and inspect every single pound note of it. It was lovely.

Unfortunately there was a fly in the ointment as well, owing to a newspaper quote the source of which we never discovered. The local council had thrown a reception for us on our first night. We seemed to get on with everybody, and it seemed that everybody had enjoyed the show. Amazingly, the following day the local paper ran a story about the show, claiming that one of the councillors had condemned it as blue. It was absurd – our show was especially designed for audiences of holidaymakers, many of whom would be families. We asked the newspaper for the name of the councillor they had quoted, but they could not tell us; so we spoke to the councillors individually, offering to remove from the show anything they thought offensive. But they were all as mystified as we were. Box office takings fell, and when the daily newspapers picked up the story they crashed. We realized then that we had made a big mistake in turning down another series of *Blackpool Night Out*. We'd said no because of those hellish journeys to and from the studios, but even they would have been preferable to being treated like outcasts in Scarborough.

Luckily all the fuss had died down by our next season in Yarmouth, which was a record-breaker. All our old friends seemed to be appearing in a show down there that year. Morecambe and Wise were there, and so were Val Doonican, Mike Yarwood and our very old mate Joe Baker. We had marvellous times together. One night we had dinner with Eric and Ernie and swapped partners, so that I did a little cabaret with Ernie and Mike had a go with Eric. It was good fun, but I think we were better suited to our normal partners. Eric was a very good friend of mine, not the least bit competitive and a very generous performer. He really entertained us at my son Ray's bar mitzvah: such a lovely man. Supper with Mike Yarwood was like being out with twenty people. He'd imitate me, Mike and Siggi, and really confuse the waiters when he turned on his Harold Wilson voice and then changed it to Frankie Howerd. Our friends were all in different shows, but luckily we all knew each other too well to worry about who was doing the better business.

In 1968, as well as a summer season at Blackpool we were invited to go to Aden to entertain the troops who were out there protecting Britain's oil interests. Practically all of them had left by the time we got there, and it felt very hairy travelling around in armoured vehicles with bombs going off too close for comfort. During a show at Aden Airport we were subjected to a surprise attack by mortar bombs. Despite the fact that the majority of the audience disappeared to try to find the terrorists responsible, we manically carried on with our act. I like to think it was courage, but actually it was sheer terror.

Part of the tour involved entertaining British troops stationed on a nearby small and backward island. The sultan sent some of his guards to see the show and when the dancing girls appeared they started to poke rifles at us. Actually they were trying to buy the girls with their guns but I thought they were about to shoot us, so I disappeared pronto.

I was relieved to get back to a safe, normal and dysentery-free Brighton summer season and later to the London Palladium, during which time we appeared in the Sophie Tucker Memorial Benefit. Jack Benny decided at the last minute to make a surprise appearance. We were very excited about meeting him, although we dreaded the idea of following his act on stage; but he put us at our ease immediately: 'I hear you two are a very funny team,' he said. We couldn't imagine how on earth he could know who we were, but we were hugely flattered. Then he reassured us that all he was going to do was to pay a simple tribute to Sophie. No doubt the incredibly warm reception he got changed his mind, and we were honoured to see this top American comedian performing so magnificently for a good half-hour. We very sensibly decided just to tell a couple of jokes when we went on. How do you follow Jack Benny? We were delighted when he appeared in our dressing room at the Palladium a few days later. He had only come in for a chat but he is such a naturally funny man that even stories about his visit to London had us in stitches.

In 1969 we took another job abroad, this time in the safer climes of Australia. Mike and I decided that we'd travel the luxury route via Bangkok and Hong Kong rather than the arduous thirty-eight-hour direct flight. It didn't take Siggi and Cassie long to realize that if we went that way we'd be apart for at least ten days longer, so we ended up on the dreaded long haul. It's not that I don't like flying – it's just that sometimes it frightens me senseless and so I tend to drink too much on the plane. While still sober I gave Mike all my cash for safe keeping, but I'd forgotten that by the time we stopped over in Beirut. Then when I put my hand in my pocket to pay for yet another brandy I nearly caused an international incident by accusing everybody of stealing my wallet.

We fell in love with Sydney. It had changed considerably since I was first there during my stint with the merchant navy when I was just seventeen – but it was still a fabulous place and a lot of fun and there always seemed to be parties going on. A journalist from the *Sunday Mirror* threw one especially for us on the night we arrived. We were so jet-lagged that we didn't remember much about it but apparently it had been marvellous – so much so that it was mentioned on the *Two-Way Family Favourites* radio programme relayed to England the next day.

Siggi and Cassie just happened to be listening and boy! did we get hell next time we spoke to them. Siggi still hadn't really calmed down even by the time I finally got home and all my attempts at peace offerings sailed out of the window one by one: toy koala bear, boomerang, fur coat.

When we made our next trip, this time to South Africa, Siggi and Cassie came with us. I wish we hadn't gone there. The whole political situation upset us enormously, and for some obscure reason our new agent, Michael Grade, had billed us as England's top Jewish comedians. We couldn't believe it when we saw our first audience, which was full of incredibly rich South African Jews expecting the kind of show that someone like Jackie Mason would give. We've never told a Jewish joke in our lives, and within seconds it was obvious that they weren't the least bit impressed by our humour. I was tempted to come straight home, but Michael Grade told us to stay and finish our bookings. The entire trip was incredibly gloomy; it rained all the time and we didn't dare refer to race or politics. In fact, we hardly dared mention that we were in South Africa at all.

While we were there we were invited to take part in a radio play which would also act as an audition for a series. It turned out to be one of the many times in my life that I have regretted not staying on longer at school. This was because we were handed the script and asked to perform it immediately. Mike was playing someone called Bernie, which threw me even more, and every time I forgot and called him Mike the director yelled at me, making me even more nervous. The whole thing was a complete fiasco, and I was so useless that it took what seemed like forever to record this half-hour play. Normally, if I'm given scripted lines in a show I'll make sure that I've learnt them well before I give the performance, but on this occasion there was no opportunity to do so – and it really showed. Needless to say we failed the audition for the series, but that was one time I was relieved not to land a job.

The horrible tour took us from Johannesburg to Durban. After a few weeks we were contacted by the hotel chain which owned the place in Johannesburg where we'd stayed. The deal with the show's producers had included an agreement that the production company would pick up our hotel tabs – only they hadn't. But the first we knew about it was when some charming representatives of the South African authorities turned up to arrest us. We tried to explain the situation, but the police, egged on by the hotel management, would have none of it. Fortunately, Mike and I always travelled with a cash reserve which was only to be used in dire emergencies. As it looked as though we were right in the middle of one we offered to pay the outstanding hotel bills with our traveller's cheques. Even the police started to sympathize with us when the hotel manager refused to accept them, insisting that we paid him in cash. Eventually, they persuaded him to take our cheques. But to add insult to injury we had to pay an additional fine before we could be released.

Money problems followed us for the rest of the tour, until in Bulawayo in Rhodesia we found ourselves once again in deep trouble. Because of their previous track record, we told the show's producers that we wouldn't perform unless we were paid up front. They said that would be no problem – but once again they let us down. They told us three times that our money would arrive, was about to arrive, had arrived. It never arrived. There were twenty of us in the show and no one had a bean other than Mike and I. Amazingly, we still had some of our 'reserve' left, which went some way towards preventing us all from starving.

When the tour came to an end, we were absolutely delighted. I'd never been so relieved to leave a place in all my life. We were virtually singing with joy at the airport until we were handed a bill for several hundred pounds to cover excess baggage. Our hearts stopped – our famous cash reserve had completely run out, and for one horrible moment we thought we wouldn't be allowed to leave the country. We were saved from this fate by an airport officer who recognized Mike and me and allowed us to board the plane without making the payment. We promised him that we would pay the bill once we got home. All in all it was a dreadful trip and I'd never want to go back.

Back in England we were asked to cover in a show in Leicester for Englebert Humperdinck, who had lost his voice through a throat infection. We agreed to do it but were pretty petrified. After all, the place was full of females all crazy about the singer. We assumed we would be booed off the stage, but the MC promised anybody who wasn't satisfied their money back. By the time we had finished the audience was with us to the point where they were yelling for more and were throwing their flowers – originally intended for Englebert – on to the stage for us.

Later that year Mike had a throat infection of his own which actually took him off stage for two weeks. We were playing the Pavilion in Bournemouth, and after the matinee he and I had a small argument about something that had happened in the act. You can snap at each other sometimes when things don't go quite right – in fact over the years we were together we must have had hundreds of such tiffs. At the time I didn't take this one any more seriously than the rest. I went back to the dressing room and assumed that he had gone to the café next door to have a puff on his pipe, but when I went to collect him fifteen minutes before our evening performance he'd disappeared. I checked with the stage door man, who told me that Mike had got into his car and driven off an hour or so before. I didn't know what to do. A few minutes later the call for the overture came and Mike was nowhere to be seen. We had a major part in the show: four spots involving sketches, dancing and a few songs, and I knew that all I could do was pull the show. I got hold of the stage manager to tell him, but then Lionel Blair appeared and said, 'Don't be ridiculous – you can't cancel the whole show. I'll do it with you. Just tell me what to say and I'll do Mike's bits.'

I knew it couldn't possibly work but didn't know what else I could do, so after talking through the sketches with Lionel I went on to the stage to announce that Mike had been taken ill and would not be appearing. The show was already half an hour late starting by then, and I told the audience that they could have their money back if they wanted to leave. Only three people got up to go, so I launched into our opening number:

> When you're feeling low
> Don't you wear a frown
> Put a smile on your choochy face
> And just go 'eeeh'.

My heart was in my boots – I felt sure the whole thing was going to be a disaster. But Lionel had been around so much when we did our act, either as choreographer or dancer in our shows, that he knew the gist of it – so in the next sketch he fed back most of Mike's lines with no trouble. I was in my long coat and bowler hat as my Mr Bowler character standing amongst the audience:

ME: 'Good evening, good evening. Has the show started?'
LIONEL: 'I'm sure I've seen you before. Weren't you in *The Planet of the Apes*? How did you get here?'
ME: 'On my uncle's ticket.'
LIONEL: 'And where's your uncle?'
ME: 'Outside looking for his ticket.'

We were word perfect. The audience loved it, so my confidence came back again.

Then in the next sketch I had to feed Lionel Mike's lines, but it still worked. It was a wedding scene where I was dressed up as the bride and Lionel was the groom. When I fell over my frock I got a big laugh; then Lionel said 'So this is it' and I said 'So soon?' Then at the hotel for the honeymoon he said, 'Would you like the bridals?' to which I answered 'Can't I just hang on to your ears?' The only thing we couldn't replace was our end music number where Mike played the clarinet, so we substituted a dance number which Lionel had choreographed anyway. It did so well that we carried on like this for another two weeks. Mike and I had also booked in for a Sunday concert at Yarmouth during this time, which I really thought I should cancel – but Lionel told me not to be so daft and we sold out.

It's unbelievable to think that I have known Lionel nearly all my life – since I was seven in fact – and strange how it worked out that almost every show that Mike and I did Lionel would be involved in as well. The simple reason was that he was the best choreographer in the business. I called him 'Mr Showbiz' because he loves it all so much. He was never happier than when wandering into Annabel's club with Sammy Davis Jnr on one arm and Liza Minnelli on the other. Sammy Davis even used to mention Lionel in his act. I was Lionel's best man at his wedding, but I'm sure he only chose me after Sammy and the rest of showbiz couldn't make it.

One of the most exciting things of my life happened to me during our time in Bournemouth: the Arsenal football team came down for a break with Bertie Mee, their manager. It was incredible to have all my heroes in one spot – Frank McLintock, George Graham, Bob Wilson, the whole squad. I've been a football fan all my life, ever since my early childhood when I used to collect cigarette cards of famous players, and I was always an Arsenal supporter. When I could afford it my agent, Joe Collins, and I had front seats in the west stand for years. So you can imagine how I felt when the team turned up *en masse* just over the road in Bournemouth. I invited them to see the show and would drive them around in my big red Rolls-Royce convertible. When I got back to London I had a party and they all came. Since then they've become very close. They even made a plaque for me, calling me Arsenal's No. 1 Fan, and gave me a football signed by the team that won the League Championship and FA Cup double in 1971. I wrote a song for them for the Cup Final in the early eighties, and coincidentally my son Ray played with an amateur team called Wingate which George Graham used to train.

Mike eventually recovered from his throat bug but now, looking back, I wonder if that episode didn't signal the beginning of our break-up. In October 1972 we were invited to make a return visit to Australia, which we were delighted to accept. Siggi couldn't come with us this time unfortunately, which was a real shame, but she had an engagement to dance in a show with Dickie Henderson.

We went to Sydney to do some television shows as well as some live appearance at the St George's Leagues Club. The Aussies were surprisingly cool about putting a television show together. We were used to having a script, rehearsing it, changing it and then rehearsing the amended script before taping – the normal way of making a television programme. In Sydney we turned up to meet the producer, who told us to come back in two days when we would record our inserts for the show. We weren't given any scripts and were convinced the whole thing was going to be a disaster. On the day we were stunned by how smoothly the whole show went – and before we knew it the taping was over. What we recorded was perfectly adequate, but it was nerve-racking to have so little rehearsal and I think I much prefer the British way of endless rehearsing.

Before our stage show one night we had supper at the Bistro, the restaurant favoured by showbiz celebrities. Donald Peers and Alfred Marks were also dining there, and before long our supposed quick pre-show meal turned into a riotous party with everybody who was anybody joining our table. Apparently Mike and I did manage to stagger to the club later that night to perform our show – taking half the restaurant with us. I can honestly say I don't recall a single thing about the meal, the show or the wild party we threw in our dressing room afterwards.

It was a very enjoyable trip and one of the last, I think, on which Mike and I were genuinely happy together. We carried on working but over the next couple of years, until we agreed to break up, our relationship deteriorated and everything became too arduous to be enjoyable any more.

7

THE FIVE-YEAR PLAN

IT had taken Mike and me thirty years of hard graft to make it to the top, but once we were there we let it destroy us. We were living it up 700 per cent. When we weren't making our television programmes we were touring the country with our stage act. We'd be away from home practically all the time working very hard, often seven days a week, and playing even harder. Wherever we were we would find the local clubs which were open the latest and become their best customers for as long as we were there. To call it too much wine, women and song wouldn't be an understatement, and foolishly we thought we could get away with it. But as ye sow so shall ye reap, as the saying goes, and it couldn't have been more true in our case. We destroyed ourselves professionally and nearly took our families down with us. Mike and I had been living in each other's pockets for years and in fact we went the way of most double acts, who are notorious for refusing to share a dressing room and hardly speaking to each other when they're not on stage. Somehow, because we're brothers, I never thought that would happen to us; but sure enough we started to argue incessantly, mainly about our act, and slowly a rift began to open between us professionally which would never heal. It's only in the last year that we've really become friends again and that was because of the cancer, both mine and his. If nothing else it teaches you how incredibly stupid you've been.

Looking back, we really started to hit the big time when Mike decided that I should wear an outsized suit. This was in the late fifties, and up until then we'd both come on stage in normal clothes, relying on our material to get us laughs. The first time I walked out with these enormous clothes on and we got a huge laugh we knew we'd hit on something good, and we capitalized on it. We would burlesque whatever or whoever was topical. We'd follow what was in the newspapers or on television and dress up like the people who were making the headlines. It could have been zoot suits, flower child outfits, Sonny and Cher (I was Cher, needless to say) or the Beatles. As soon as we appeared with Beatles haircuts and guitars strapped round us, singing 'It's Been a Hard Day's Night', the audience would fall about. We'd wear silly clothes for other sketches as well, more often than not with me dressed up as a woman. I'm not suggesting that we were the only people who ever used costumes – Norman Wisdom's whole career was based on his most famous character, who wore a tight-fitting suit, and Morecambe and Wise would always dress up if the sketch required it. Dressing up has always played a big part in comedy and still does, and it had become really important in our act.

But for some reason Mike decided he didn't want to wear silly clothes any more. So the sketch writers would write something which required us to appear in costume and he would refuse to do it. When, during the early seventies, we made Michael Grade our agent, he supported Mike's way of thinking and told me that I had to dress in an evening suit and black tie. All of a sudden the things which had made us successful were being questioned, but nothing was replacing them. The whole image was going – you could feel it falling apart.

There was a lot of bad feeling and pettiness between Mike and me at that time, and it affected our families as well. Siggi and Cassie, Mike's wife, who'd been practically inseparable, began to drift apart. Mike and I disagreed on virtually everything: when we should take holidays, where we should work, what we wanted to do, even whether we should change agents. At one stage, before we left Joe Collins, who'd been our agent almost from the beginning, another agent offered us £40,000 to become his clients. I refused to leave Joe, so that created another row. Other people started to get involved, too. Friends and production staff at the studios where we were working would say to me, 'What do you want him for? He's nothing but a hindrance. Why don't you go on your own? You'd be much better off.' It all seemed so ludicrous. We were more successful than we'd ever been, but it was tearing us apart and destroying our families.

I have to admit that our television shows had been going downhill; but strangely enough, after we'd overcome the problems about dressing up, our stage act got better and better. We really did work well together, to the point where I could slip in something completely new without telling Mike and his surprise would be as funny to the audience as my stunt. One night, we were halfway through our act when suddenly the lights went out. Mike started rushing around trying to get someone to fix them, while I just stood stock still. The music started up and a spotlight was shone on me. I was handed an enormous cane which I swept about the stage, and a cigar was lowered into my hand. A lighted match appeared as if from nowhere from the side of the stage and I lit the cigar. It was exactly like the Hamlet cigar advert which was showing at the time and it went down a bomb, as much because of Mike's surprise as anything.

Despite the good times, though, Mike and I were coming to an end and we both knew it. Eventually we had to admit it to each other as well. It came to a head one day when we were at Heathrow airport of all places, on our way to do a television show in Canada. Mike had Cassie with him. Siggi and Ray were coming with me. Suddenly Mike and I started to fight like we'd never fought before, all over some booking that he didn't want to do. He said he'd had enough of always being on the move.

We were at the end of our tether and so I said, 'Okay, let's break up.' We agreed to split, but made a deal that we'd keep the act going for another five years so that we could each work out what we were going to do with our futures. It sounds odd, giving ourselves all that time to split, but that was because we knew it would break our father's heart. When he died in 1975, I knew it was the end of Mike and me. Our relationship got steadily worse during that time. Already we'd broken up socially. Mike mixed with the business set – all Harrods and champagne – while Siggi and I were pretty basic, spending our time with showbiz people. The popular *Pig 'n' Whistle* television show we did in Toronto went off all right but our personal lives were in a mess. Mike was having problems with his family and I was miserable, wanting to confess the times that I'd behaved badly to Siggi but not having the courage.

Things didn't improve much over the next five years, either. As well as our personal problems, our act was getting worse. The drive and enthusiasm just weren't the same as they had been when we were striving to get to the top. We'd already lost interest to the point where we just wanted to know 'How much?' and 'Where do you want us to stand on stage?', and now it was a matter of trying to get through the bookings when our hearts weren't in it. We were very lazy, not rehearsing and hardly ever introducing new material. All we were interested in was living the high life, though not with each other. After a couple of years of this arrangement the tension became unbearable. We were playing a club in Birmingham one night with the Deep River Boys when there was some aggravation. It ended up with Mike and me nearly coming to blows, and it was only the hard efforts of our friends that kept us apart. I was staying with Lenny Smith, a very old friend whom I'd known for more than thirty years, and he took me back to his house where I just sat and shook drinking brandy. He told me he was going to call Siggi, but I said, 'No, she'll go mad.' He phoned anyway and she drove all the way up to Birmingham that night, arriving at

5 a.m. I told her I couldn't imagine going on stage with Mike after what had happened, but through her persuasion I did. The next night, throughout the whole act we never talked to each other or looked at each other – we just said the words. There was no feeling, no love on the stage and no smiles – it was dreadful. It was very hard after that. Staying together was like living through a marriage that you know is on the rocks. It happens. It happens all the time. It's hard to hold on to success. We were at the top and we abused what we had.

As time went on and the full realization of what our agreement meant hit me, I started to wonder what on earth I was going to do. Somehow I couldn't contemplate a future without show business. That had been my life for thirty years and I couldn't imagine doing anything else, but going it alone was a petrifying prospect. I wasn't able to think of a single comic who had survived the break-up of a double act – even Jerry Lewis hadn't done as well after he split with Dean Martin. He'd carried on working and making movies, but they weren't as good. I really didn't know what I was going to do. I wasn't a stand-up comedian – I needed someone or something else to bounce off. Eric Morecambe was the same. He knew he wouldn't have survived a break-up with Ernie because his comedy, like mine, all worked through other people or situations, as it did so well for him with André Previn and Glenda Jackson. Standing up and telling jokes, like Jimmy Tarbuck does so brilliantly, is a completely different form of comedy and I'm simply not good enough for it. I mean when you're used to someone saying to you, 'Now if I say I want what I want when I want it, what would you say?' and you answer, 'Well, I'd tell you that you'll get what I've got when I get it', how can you suddenly do that on your own? It just doesn't work, so although I knew I wanted to stay in the business after Mike and I broke up, I didn't know how I was going to manage it and I was scared stiff. It was like going from success into oblivion as far as I was concerned. Mike's family didn't help: they told me how they didn't think I'd survive, that I'd be nothing without him.

By the time we got to our summer season in Skegness two years before the final split, it was obvious that we weren't even trying for our audiences and so they gave us what we deserved – they didn't bother to come and see us. The place was empty. I feel ashamed now to think that we could have behaved like that. After all, it wasn't the audience's fault that we didn't get on any more. After that episode I was relieved that we were breaking up, and I think Mike was as well.

Then things started to change. About six months before the end, Philip Jones at Thames Television called me and asked if I'd like to do a situation comedy for him. I didn't have to be asked twice – I was over the moon. Not only was it work for me as a solo comic but a sitcom could be the perfect vehicle for me, giving me something to work with and bounce off. I knew by this time that Mike had his own plans. He was going to take his family to live in Miami, where he intended to go into partnership with a friend and sell machinery. He'd always loved the way of life in Florida, the constant sunshine and partying, so he was happy about the decision. I was too until our last summer season at Sandown in the Isle of Wight. At first I was dreading it, expecting more empty houses and disappointment, but something happened to us that week and we performed brilliantly – at least as well as we'd ever done before. We had four or five spots in the show, and each one was better than the last. The theatre was packed out every night, and by the end the audience would be screaming and cheering. It was incredible, but Mike and I still weren't speaking. We weren't even lodging in the same place. He was staying in Sandown with his family, but I used to take the midnight ferry after the show and stay the night in Southsea or drive back home to London; so apart from the show itself we didn't spend any time together at all.

Siggi and Ray drove down with me for the last show. That

was on 16 September 1978. It was hard to believe it was actually coming to an end, despite having had five years to plan for it. As we got to the theatre that night the House Full boards were out, and I remember saying, 'Is this really the end? It should be the beginning.' We were on the crest of a wave, and there we were throwing it all away.

We got on stage and the place just seemed to erupt. When I made the announcement that it was our last performance together there were standing ovations, tons of photographers, tears and sadness. I presented Mike with a glass bowl which I'd had engraved with: 'To the Best Straight Man in the World'. Then that was it – it was over. Mike walked off to the left of the stage and I walked off to the right; I got into my car with Siggi and Ray and drove to the ferry, and Mike went off to a party with a few friends. He left England for the States a short time later and, other than one phone call, I didn't speak to him again for many years. It was unbelievable, as though the last thirty years hadn't happened; but there was no going back. Sometimes you get to the stage when enough is enough, and this time we'd reached it. It was very sad and very painful at the time, but if we had carried on I wonder where we would be. We'd be quite old men by now and we've been too ill, the pair of us. We just wouldn't have the energy to do the kind of act we used to do – it would be hopeless. Perhaps it was for the best.

8

BY MYSELF

THE comedy for Thames Television was called *It's Bernie*, and I was due to start filming the Monday after my final performance with Mike. I'd been thinking a lot about the best character for me and had come up with the idea of having a big dog. I'd envisaged an Irish wolfhound which would go everywhere and do everything with me but always get me into trouble. I would be a not very successful person who had to travel a lot in a small Fiat car with the dog's head sticking out of its open roof. I would land in scrapes, for instance if I went to get digs and the landlady said, 'No women and definitely no dogs' I'd have to smuggle the dog out of the car and through a ground-floor window and under the bed without her knowing. The idea wasn't exactly to replace Mike with a dog, but to give me some kind of hook because I was very nervous about starting again on my own. John Ammonds, the producer of the show, had already told me that he didn't want any of my Mr Bowler routine with the 'eeeehs' and 'choochy faces' or teeth and eyes: he wanted acting. I was to learn the words and stick exactly to the script, so to say that I was terrified would be an understatement.

Anyway Thames, in its wisdom, eventually decided that *It's Bernie* would be a sketch show rather than a sitcom. They liked the idea of the dog, however, so I tried to think of a name for it.

Some years before, Ray used to go skiing regularly to a small

77

resort outside Stuttgart where he kept meeting some drunk who, whenever he got sozzled, had the strange habit of calling everybody Schnorbitz. Mike and I had started picking the name up in our act: 'I studied at the Consèrvatoire in Paris under Professor Schnorbitz, a very eminent musician' etc. Ray suggested that it would be the perfect name for the dog, and once we'd worked out how to spell it we had a big name plaque made to hang around her neck. In fact I didn't meet Schnorbitz until the first day of filming as she was hired expecially for the programme, and so I was surprised to find that she wasn't an Irish wolfhound but a massive great St Bernard. We seemed to get on well straightaway, but unfortunately her first spot of filming wasn't a great success. Thames had supplied a Panther car for us to film the title sequence in – rather more upmarket than the Fiat I'd pictured – and the idea was that I should drive around Windsor Great Park singing 'It's Bernie, saying "Hello" to you. It's Bernie . . .' and so on, with Schnorbitz sitting next to me in the passenger seat. Everything was fine until she decided to shift around between takes and instead of jumping on to the seat she landed on the gear lever and broke it.

Although Schnorbitz didn't appear in any of the sketches we had a sit-down routine at the beginning and end of each programme where I'd tell jokes about her and feed her sausages. It was such a relief not to have to stand out there on my own, but she was a pretty tough audience: if she wasn't satisfactorily entertained she'd fall asleep. By the end of the series she became exceedingly popular and I was delighted that I'd chosen such a good partner. The sketches were also very good, and so I was starting to feel more confident. I had marvellous writers, top actors and special guests like Joan Collins and Diana Dors, both of whom were old friends. Di played my mother in a sketch about kids at school. It's great working with old friends. You don't have to try and build a rapport – it's already there. I'd known Di since we were both in our teens. She used to come into the Havana coffee bar in

Gerrard Street, where most aspiring stars seemed to end up at one time or another, and even then she was a stunning blonde. You knew, just to look at her, that she'd make it. I had a lot of good times with Di and her husband, Alan. She was responsible for my first foray into soft porn movies. You'll be relieved to hear that I didn't take my clothes off; I just played a landlord and I didn't realize till after the shooting that it was soft porn – honest! Many years later she and I helped Des O'Connor out on the pilot of his chat show for Thames Television, and it went so well that we were booked for the first real show. That went well too, but afterwards she told me that she wasn't feeling too good – she thought she had cancer. Sadly, just a couple of months later she died. It was a terrible loss. She was such a lovely lady and one of the many people I've known whom the dreadful disease has taken a hold of.

So all in all *It's Bernie* seemed to be a real success, but I'd had to get used to a very different way of working. When I was making television programmes with Mike I'd been used to a lot more freedom. In fact Philip Jones, who produced us, encouraged it. He didn't reshoot if we corpsed, because normally the audience loved it, and he would never dream of stopping us ad-libbing just because he thought a light might not be in the right place. If he thought a script wasn't up to scratch, he'd say, 'Do something. Go out and muck around – don't worry about the words.' So of course I had all the confidence in the world, knowing that whatever I did was likely to be approved. But *It's Bernie* was far more rigid; if I wandered even slightly from the script, we'd reshoot. However, I still think the series contained some of the funniest sketches I've ever done. Siggi's favourite is the one where I played a butler with broken legs who had to deliver a bottle of wine on crutches – I was falling all over the place, of course. In my own favourite I was an air force pilot with a bust which everybody else was trying to ignore until eventually it got in the way of the controls. At this stage the commanding officer felt he had to say something to me about it, and I had to play dumb as though I didn't realize there was anything strange about me. It was an immensely popular series – people would stop me in the street during transmission to tell me they loved it and that they watched it every week.

Before *It's Bernie* came on air I was booked for the Christmas 1978 pantomime at the Theatre Royal in Bath. For the previous twenty years I'd always been top of the bill or thereabouts, but at Bath I was fifth. Actually it was very good for me. It helped me learn how to be on stage without Mike, but all those years at the top had left their mark and I started off in my usual way, telling the director how I wanted things done and trying to run the show as I'd done with Mike. Unfortunately I hadn't yet grasped that I was an absolute nobody in this show. Before long I was told: 'What's it got to do with you? Do you realize who you are and where you are? It's really nothing to do with you.' I hated it, of course, but I played my part really well and, although I wasn't the star of the show, I was a real hit. I also hadn't lost my other bill-topping habit of staying at the best hotels, throwing parties and inviting people back for drinks. The problem when you're only fifth is that it's costing you more than you're earning.

I came back from pantomime to a second series of *It's Bernie* and after that Siggi and I took a holiday at Eilat in Israel. We stayed in a hotel where Tony Curtis was making a movie. I remember opening the papers one day and seeing that *It's Bernie* was Number Nine in the Top Twenty and I was running around the hotel showing everyone and saying, 'Look, that's my name there. I'm Number Nine.' I felt wonderful and thought that I'd really cracked it; it didn't really worry me that I was disturbing the filming.

I suppose I should have realized that things were going too well. While we'd been making the programmes, Thames had been bringing in people like Hywel Bennet and Jim Davidson, their new signings, to see me work and telling them, 'You must see this fellow perform. Watch how he talks to the audience and see how warm he is.' So of course I was terribly chuffed; I thought I'd really arrived, but unfortunately they'd arrived and I was out. We didn't make any more *It's Bernie*s. I couldn't understand why not, because the show was doing so well. I still don't understand it to this day.

A few months later Thames offered me *Big Top Variety*, an entertainment show set in a circus ring. We only made three programmes a year as they were so expensive, but they were very successful. They were always Number One or Two in the ratings, but at first I didn't think that I was very good. I had to feel my way around, playing in a big top with Schnorbitz, but each year I seemed to do a little better and my confidence started to build up again. By the third series I was hiring straight men to do gags with and joking around with the audience; I felt like Bernie on stage again. My only problem was Schnorbitz. Otherwise known as Brandy, she belonged to a young girl in Surrey and was brought to the studios at Teddington by an animal hire company. It wasn't a very satisfactory arrangement for me because every evening she'd be taken home after we'd finished working, and really I prefer to spend as much time as possible with the person or dog I'm performing with. It ended up not being very satisfactory for the owner either, as everybody started to call her dog Schnorbitz instead of Brandy and it upset her. Thames found another St Bernard to replace Brandy, but I decided that it was ridiculous to hire a dog and so I tried to buy her. The company were having none of it at first as they made a lot of money out of her, but eventually they let her go for £1000. That Schnorbitz stayed with me till she died aged eight and a half in 1988. She was a wonderful dog with a beautiful nature and is sorely missed. Now we're on to Schnorbitz Three and she's taken to stardom like a duck to water!

Over the three years of *Big Top* I don't think a week ever went by without me being on television, even when *Big Top* was off the air. I was always doing *Punchlines* with Lennie Bennett or *Celebrity Squares* or the breakfast programmes. Jeremy Beadle once said to me, 'Something strange happened today – Bernie Winters wasn't on television!' I was forever travelling the country to Tyne Tees in Newcastle or to Grampian Television in Scotland, and I think I did more *Give Us a Clue*s than anyone other than the resident panel. I was really enjoying myself. I even did a commercial for Batchelor's soups. I played a chicken and, to be honest, for the £15,000 they paid me I would have played anything. And so, feeling happier now about being on television on my own, I decided I would take on the theatre too.

I'd seen a lot of comedians like Max Wall and Jimmy Jewell move on to straight theatre in later life, so when I was offered a starring role in a farce at Yarmouth I grabbed it. It seemed like a good idea at the time because it would extend my repertoire. Little did I know it would be so dreadful! I can't even remember what it was called, but that's not surprising – you tend to try and forget nightmares. Anyway, the play had already been touring for a while with Sid James and Barbara Windsor. The character which I took over from Sid was a television star with teenage kids but no wife. The part Linda Barron took over from Barbara was the housekeeper who looked after the unruly family. It was set in hippy days, which was the first mistake – it should have been punk by the time that I was in it – and involved a lot of comings and goings with young people, their boyfriends and girlfriends as well as the Swedish au pair. I added a scene at the beginning where the TV star tells his dog how to behave on stage so that Schnorbitz had a role, and every night I would sit on stage with her by my side looking out over an audience, if you can call it that, of about fifteen people – most of whom I think had come in to shelter from the rain. They definitely weren't the least bit interested in what was happening on stage, and you can't blame them. The play was due to run for ten weeks, and when something is that bad and you know you can't break your contract you half hope that something drastic will happen like the theatre burning down. The building itself was no great shakes – in fact it would have been kinder to burn it down and put it out of its misery. The walls were like tissue paper, so that every passing fire engine or police siren could be heard during the performance. My dressing room, which was more like a small cupboard really, particularly when Schnorbitz was squeezed in there with me, backed on to the street where mothers would be screaming at their kids: 'Eat yer chips and stop snivelling!' Or courting couples would smooch against the wall or, worst of all, drunks pee up it – and I had the luxury of being able to hear, in precise detail, every moment of it.

At least I had the dogs. I'd rented a bungalow for the run and had brought Butch, my boxer, down as well as Schnorbitz. It was nice to have them both there, but maybe it wasn't sensible. Butch hated Schnorbitz. I don't know if he was jealous because she was the star, but he'd try and take a bite out of her whenever he thought no one was looking. St Bernards are real softies and don't fight back, so this went on all their lives together. Even when Butch got old and lost his teeth he'd still try and gum her. So life at the bungalow consisted of me trying to keep the peace between them, mainly by keeping them apart. They slept in separate rooms, had separate mealtimes and had to be taken on separate walks. Every morning I'd take Schnorbitz along the beach. She loved the sea, and the holidaymakers used to enjoy watching her play with the waves. I'd sign a million autographs for them but that still didn't persuade them to come to the show – they weren't that daft, unfortunately. We soon had a regular route. Along the beach, then tea for me at the café and an ice cream for her. One morning we were tucking in at the café when I saw this 'thing' pass by along the top of the promenade. It was small but unmistakable – Butch's knobbly tail. He'd managed to escape from the bungalow. Within seconds he'd found us in the café. Schnorbitz made a dash for the back door and Butch flew after her, sending tables flying. 'Get those bloody dogs out of here!' was the last thing I heard as I followed in hot pursuit. Needless to say, we didn't dare show our faces in there again.

When you're in a really bad show, other stars in other shows in the same town stay away from you – it's like they've heard that you've got the plague and they don't want to catch it. So my time in Yarmouth was pretty lonely. It was odd, because my *Big Top Variety* shows were on television by this time and doing very well, but it didn't seem to make any difference. So it was a great relief when my old friend Joan Collins, her children and husband Ron Kass called up to say they were coming down for a week. I got them into the Carlton Hotel and things started to look up. At least there'd be five in the audience!

Joanie and I go back a long way. We'd known each other ever since her and Jackie's father, Joe Collins, had become Mike's and my agent, and as Joe was also like a father to me Jackie and Joan were almost like sisters. Joe really looked after me and sometimes I really needed it. He'd advance me money when I ran out or my car broke down and I couldn't pay for it, which happened not infrequently. And Joe and his first wife, Elsa, threw memorable parties which always seemed to be full of celebrities. And of course I knew Anthony Newley, Joan's first husband, well too: I'd made that movie, *Idle on Parade*, with him before they got married and he was a very good friend. Jackie used to pick my brains for all the showbiz gossip at the nightclub Tramp. She always says that the time she spent at that club, getting the stories and watching the comings and goings, was the inspiration for her early novels. I can well believe it – quite a lot happens at Tramp! So we were all very close – in fact it was Joe who sent Joan down to Yarmouth for a holiday.

Joanie was great; she'd come and spend the afternoon at the bungalow every day and we'd sit and commiserate with each other. She'd let me cry on her shoulder about the dreadful play, and I'd let her cry on mine because at that time her career was slow. After all, she'd normally be in Hollywood for her holidays, not Yarmouth. She'd sit in the garden with her peaked dealer's hat and huge comic's trousers like Eric Morecambe used to wear and I'd tell her that she could hardly expect to be taken seriously as a sex symbol looking like that. Shortly afterwards she started the really successful Martini commercials with Leonard Rossiter and she sent me a case of the stuff in memory of our summer together. The next time I saw her was after her daughter Katy's dreadful car accident. I visited them in hospital with Schnorbitz, and we put on a little show for her.

The only other person I spent any time with then was Russ Abbot. He was playing the Britannica Pier and going down a bomb, but he was struggling at that time with the prospect of breaking away from the Black Abbots – Russ was going through exactly what I'd experienced in my break-up with Mike. We used to weep into our beer together after our respective shows, and because I was depressed about the play I'd warn him about going it alone. He must have thought I was completely mad – and look what's happened to Russ!

The only night I really enjoyed being on stage throughout that summer run was when Butch visited us in the theatre. Having perfected his Houdini act, he'd escaped from the bungalow and found us at the theatre. He arrived ten minutes before curtain up so, although Schnorbitz was none too pleased, there was little I could do other than shut him in our dressing room while we went to do the play. The set was quite simple – it was supposed to be my living room. There was the couch in the middle which I sat on next to Schnorbitz, a fireplace to the left and behind us some steps leading up to the front door which was painted on to the backcloth. I'd just launched into my speech to Schnorbitz about how to behave in a television studio – and I might as well have been talking to myself because the few people in the audience weren't paying much attention – when suddenly there was a sound of things breaking and ripping over by the fireplace. Within seconds Butch broke through it and on to the set. The normally docile Schnorbitz flew off the couch and ran round the stage, hotly pursued by Butch, and all I could see was the stage manager's arms coming through the fireplace like free-floating limbs, desperately trying to grab Butch. Schnorbitz was obviously fooled by the picture on the backcloth because she shot up the steps and crashed through the fake front door with Butch just nano-seconds behind her. I didn't know what to do. Nobody came out and stopped the play or anything and so, as I finally had the audience's attention, I just carried on with my speech – Schnorbitz-less, the set in tatters around me and with these weird arms flailing through what was left of the fireplace. That was an enjoyable night.

Even the management got fed up. One night some guy in the audience started reeling down the aisle and shouting at us on the stage. I thought it was a heckler and I was quite pleased – it was the most interest the audience had shown all the time we'd been there. He was going on about how nobody on the stage was really trying – they were all lazy except for me, and the show was a disaster. I was just getting ready to have a go at him when I suddenly realized it was the theatre manager. He was somewhat tired and emotional and wanted to take the show off, which would have been an act of mercy. Unfortunately his family came to the rescue and kept it open.

It was my own fault, really. It was far too soon for me to take the lead part in a play – after all, it was my first one. I should have asked for a smaller role so that I could spend time learning the craft rather than jumping straight into the deep end. Instead I fell for the oldest trick in the book – I'd done two successful comedy series for television and so I thought, like the play's producers, that people were bound to come and see me in a play. But of course they didn't – nobody'd ever heard of Bernie Winters the actor. So the producers didn't make billions of pounds and I was suffering from a bad case of shattered confidence.

I felt a lot safer in pantomime, so that Christmas I went to Wolverhampton to appear in *Aladdin*. Unfortunately, while it wasn't the box office disaster that Yarmouth had been it suffered from the fact that the man who put it on had, to my mind, no conception of what it was to produce a pantomime. My entrance in the first act was forty-five minutes after the curtain went up, which you don't do to the top of the bill. You've got to get him or her on quickly before everybody else has been on and done every conceivable thing that you can do in a panto. The audience have usually paid to see the star, so they feel cheated as well. Anyway, on about week seven I arrived at the theatre for the Saturday matinee to find bailiffs there putting chains all round the doors. 'What's going on?' I asked. I knew I hadn't been paid for two weeks, but I didn't realize that the brewery, the electricity people and the gas board hadn't been paid either. Despite the bailiffs, the manager ordered me to do the show. I pointed out that the audience couldn't get into the theatre. I didn't know what to do so I rang Joe Collins, who told me that as I hadn't been paid that week I should get out, so I packed up my dressing room and left. Showbiz is a funny old game, as Jimmy Greaves would say. It goes from success to disaster. I don't know anyone whose career has always run up, up, up. One minute it goes crash bang and the next you're being told, 'Ah, you were wonderful.'

But my experience of the theatre so far hadn't put me off. The following year I was offered the part of Oscar in a tour of *The Odd Couple* by Neil Simon. Malcolm Knight was the producer and Pete Murray was going to play Felix, so I was delighted to accept; I love Pete – he's a super actor and a guiding light. He really took care of me on that tour and stopped all my shenanigans. In fact he wouldn't let me go out at all, and although it was good for me I used to get bored out of my mind and would drive all the way home to London after a performance from places as far away as Chesterfield. I really couldn't stand staying in hotels without anything to do. I remember in Taunton Pete said to me, 'You've got to stay the week. You can't keep driving home every night.' I had my big Silver Spur Rolls-Royce at the time and the journeys were costing me more in petrol than I was earning, so I did stay the week. I'd say to him after the show, 'Can't we go and have a drink tonight or go to a club?' 'No,' he'd say sternly, and take me back to the hotel by the scruff of the neck.

The following week we were in Billingham, just outside Middlesborough. I drove up on the Monday with Siggi. There was a nice hotel next to the theatre but I knew I couldn't stay there – it was too dead for me. I did the play that night, got in the car and drove back to London. It was a hell of a long way and Siggi told me that if I did that every day I'd end up killing myself. So I packed my golf clubs in the boot and stayed the week – in Newcastle, though, not Billingham.

Pete and I played golf every day: we were both learning together. In fact, Pete had been playing for years but hadn't got very far because he's got no patience. He had the oldest clubs I've ever seen, which was just as well. I remember one day when every time he hit the ball he was so disgusted with himself he shouted, 'Bloody hell!' in his terribly posh voice and threw the club away. When we got to the seventh tee he suddenly declared, very theatrically and mopping his brow, 'I can't possibly play any more.'

'But it's only the seventh hole,' I said.

He went all sheepish. 'I've got no clubs left. I've thrown them all away.' Then from every direction on the golf course people came up to us waving clubs and asking, 'Have you lost a club?' So in the end poor old Pete was forced to finish the game.

Unfortunately he had to leave the play before the end of the tour – he'd been signed up by LBC to present one of their radio shows. I really missed him – he's such a gentleman and so intelligent. The actor who took over the Felix role turned in a completely different performance – he played it like the dame in pantomime, which threw me a bit. I was playing Oscar, the Walter Matthau part in the movie, and, in the circumstances I was really pleased with the way I was doing it. Every expense was spared in this production: the set was lousy, we had to wear our own clothes – I wore a baseball hat that Ray had brought me from New York – and we didn't even have understudies, so I thought that considering everything I wasn't at all bad. It wasn't a particularly successful run, mainly because Neil Simon isn't good box office in the provinces, but it was hugely enjoyable.

I must admit that I was still a bit in awe of the theatre and particularly of the actors, who are usually so deadly serious about 'The Piece' and 'The Part'. I couldn't imagine anyone fooling around on stage or letting things get out of hand. Little did I know. When we got to the Gordon Craig Theatre in Stevenage at the end of the run the guy who played the American cop was late arriving one night. I was sitting in my dressing room getting made up when Bill, the small, elderly company manager, came in to tell me the news. Fifteen minutes had already been called and so we were in a bit of a fix. 'Oh, no,' I said. 'What can we do? We don't have an understudy.'

'No,' he said thoughtfully. Suddenly he announced, 'I'll do it.'

'What?' I said. 'But you can't – you don't know the words.'

'Well,' he said, 'I'll take the script with me.'

I was gobsmacked. 'But he's four times your size and the costume won't fit you.'

'I'll wear this,' he said, pointing at the comfy grey cardigan he had on.

The farcical possibilities suddenly struck me and I said, 'All right, then. By all means let's have a go at it.'

Now *The Odd Couple* is set in deepest Brooklyn, and the cast need heavy New York accents. On this night the music starts, the curtain goes up and four guys are on stage, sitting around playing poker. Budweiser beer and Coke cans sit on the table and the guys are warming up, getting ready to gamble. I'm still off stage in 'the kitchen', making them all sandwiches. One of the men turns to our stand-in and asks, 'How many cards d'ya wan', Ernie?', at which point Bill rummages through his script to find the right page and then says, in perfect Cockney, 'I'll 'ave two, please.' How the other guys on stage managed to carry on I don't know – I was in tears in the wings. And it got worse. Someone else talks to the old guy. 'You sure you wan' two cards, Ernie?' Bill sits and stares at the script and says, 'No, I won' 'ave two. Gets up and moves to settee . . . . What?' He'd been reading the stage directions.

The audience is watching in total confusion when I make my entrance with a huge pile of sandwiches. 'Who wants a double decker corn on rye. Who wants pastrami? And there's one for you, Ernie.' I stick a sandwich on his plate and I know that he doesn't know if he's on the moon or on stage in Stevenage, so I push him over to the settee and tell him, 'This is where you say: "When's Felix comin' round?" Okay?' By now I can hardly speak myself for the tears streaming down my face.

It went on like this for the whole of the first act until the curtain came down and the poor fellow could get off stage. He was as white as a sheet. Normally his job was to make sure the scenery was okay and then be off even before the curtain went up. I don't think he'd ever seen the play. He enjoyed it, though, after he'd got over the shock. What the audience thought I'll never know, especially when the second half started and the proper actor arrived: suddenly an enormous guy in full cop's uniform was sitting there – still called Ernie! That to me was like the Mike and Bernie shows again; I hadn't believed it could happen in the straight theatre, and I really enjoyed it when it did.

A couple of years later I went into a thriller aptly named *Whodunnit?* The script was huge and my part, the chief inspector of police, was about two-thirds of it. Unfortunately my agent had forgotten to tell me when rehearsals started and so I'd merrily gone on holiday. It was only when I rang home to see how Schnorbitz was that I found out I should have been on stage. I felt dreadful, because I was trying to take the acting bit really seriously. I'd been studying Rod Steiger to see how to use my hands and arms and develop more facial expressions – a lot of good it did me! Anyway, not only was this play hugely long but my part was full of words that I'd never heard of before, like 'polysyllabic'. I still don't know what it means. By the time I got home I had four days to learn it before we opened in Dartford. The rest of the cast was really fed up with me because they had to come in specially every morning for me to rehearse. On the first night I only knew 60 per cent of the script and had to improvise the rest. I'd be rambling on, trying to follow the story, while the other actors looked at me as if to say, 'What's he doing? Why doesn't he stop talking?' Eventually I learned it through doing it, and by the end I thought I'd done rather well. Even the writer said I was good in it.

Luckily I wasn't the only one who screwed up. There was a Hungarian actor in the play who used to be the head waiter in *Crossroads*, and during the performance he was to be offered a brandy and soda by the butler. One night the butler asked him if he wanted a brandy and tonic instead, and he flipped. Now this is a heavy drama, a murder story involving a body with his head chopped off. And this actor, absolutely thrown by the butler saying 'tonic' instead of 'soda', walked to the front of the stage, threw his hands in the air and started to rave at the audience, 'Did you hear that? Did you hear what he said? He's given me the wrong line.' There were eight other actors on the stage, dumbstruck, while he carried on: 'I have no idea what to do. I don't know where I am. I really know nothing at all. I shall have to go.' And with that he walked off the stage. I mean this is a play in a theatre – it's not as though you can do a retake like in a TV studio, and it really wouldn't have mattered if the butler had said brandy and arsenic.

Anyway, then it was my turn. We were playing Peterborough and part of the set was a very narrow, curling staircase. At one point four of us are on stage and I say, 'Here I am, Chief Inspector Burns from CID Scotland Yard. I was dining with Chief Superintendent Leary last evening and he suggested that I come and sort out this problem that you're having here.' Then I point to one of them and say, 'And you, don't be so polysyllabic.' This particular night I pointed just as the butler came down the staircase, and my arm sent the tray of drinks flying. Well, I had a brainstorm. It was like being in revue again and I started on the old slapstick routine of throwing drinks and trays around. Then Jack Douglas joined in and soda syphons were flying and everyone was getting soaked. The whole thing turned into chaos and I had both the cast and the audience at the Embassy Theatre roaring with laughter. We had twenty minutes of bedlam and then of course we had to revert to the play, but no one there that night will ever forget it. You hear about actors corpsing on stage in *Hamlet*, but before my experiences I never really believed it happened. I thought it was just for summer seasons or pantomimes, but it happens in the straight theatre as well. When it does the audience loves it, and so do I.

Meanwhile I was appearing in pantomime at Christmas. Following my not too successful stint as top of the bill in *Aladdin* at Wolverhampton I'd decided to spend a couple of years finding my feet as second or third billing. That was actually wonderful experience for me, and I was free to enjoy myself as I didn't have the final responsibility for the success of the show. One year I played Widow Twanky to Su Pollard's Aladdin at the Richmond Theatre in Surrey. Su's lovely to work with. She's always enthusiastic, and when she turns up at the theatre in a duffel coat and clutching a bag of oranges you know she's not playing the star. Each day she'd go to everyone's dressing room and say, "Hello, chuck. How are you today? Going to be a great show tonight – best ever. Here's to it, luv."

One night a couple of friends from Thames Television, Brian Klein and Maurice Leonard, came to see the show. I knew them through various television programmes I had made with them, but they'd actually come down on this occasion to check out the theatre in preparation for Su's *This Is Your Life*. The idea was that she would be surprised with the big red book during the curtain call and then be whisked off to the Thames Television Studios at Teddington.

In order to make it look absolutely natural Maurice, Brian and I planned to have dinner after the performance, and I invited Su to join us. Of course Schnorbitz came too. We went to a local Italian restaurant that Su knew: she took us via a short cut which led to the back of the restaurant, and we had to go through the kitchen to get to it. All would have been well but for the fact that there was a kitchen cat. Within moments Schnorbitz was chasing the cat round the kitchen until they disappeared behind a cupboard, and then all you could see were balls of fur flying out accompanied by some dreadful screeching noises. The cat shot out through a window to safety, and amazingly the restaurant manager still let us eat there.

I went on to top the bill as Widow Twanky in various performances of *Aladdin* around the country after that. Somehow I'd managed to learn all the complicated costume changes and the fine art of outrageous stage make-up, including enormous wigs that stand at least a foot high from the top of your head.

During this time I met up with Mike again. He'd phoned me before he left for America when he saw one of the first *It's Bernie* shows on television and told me that he wasn't too keen on it. After that I hadn't seen or spoken to him for years. Then suddenly one day I was driving through Regent's Park and passed him coming the other way. For a moment I just carried on, but then I realized how crazy that was and turned round to try to catch him up.

Eventually I drew up beside him by Lord's Cricket Ground and there he was, just the same as ever. He always had a book, a pencil and a pipe, and that day was no different. He was scribbling away in his notebook and puffing away on his pipe. 'Oh hello, hello. I'm just writing my book,' he said as though we'd only been apart for a few hours rather than a few years. He got out of the car and we walked for a while through the park, chatting about what we were doing. I told him about the pantomime I was in and he told me that he'd given up the machinery business in Miami and was now involved in an assortment of projects: real estate, nightclubs and writing a biography of the great American boxing trainer Angelo Dundee. We chatted as though nothing had really happened and I felt better for it. Then we said our goodbyes.

A few months later I discovered through my sister Sylvia that Mike was back in England and in hospital in Purley, Surrey. I went straight over to see him and he was shocked to see me. I had no idea what was wrong with him, and all he would say was that he hadn't been too well and was having a check-up. He'd always been very cloak-and-dagger, unlike me – I've always been an open book. So it wasn't until much later, and not from him, that I discovered he had cancer. I was truly surprised and felt very sorry for him, but Sylvia explained that so long as he had regular treatment his illness was containable. I realized then that he must have been undergoing one of these treatments when I saw him in hospital.

On his next visit to England Mike brought Cassie, and Siggi and I threw a party for them. It was like the old days again, with friends like Micky, the late Matt Monro's wife, and we watched videos of us and Matt performing and cried and cried together. We had a sad but quite wonderful night and I thought that Mike and I would be as close as we'd ever been, but when he and Cassie went back to America we drifted apart again. After that we didn't see each other until Mike found out that I had cancer as well.

9

SCHNORBITZ SUPERSTAR

I COULDN'T have made a better choice of partner than Schnorbitz. I mean she might not have been too good at feed lines but she was absolutely adorable and went straight to the audiences' hearts. It wasn't long before she got so famous that we practically disappeared under mountains of her fanmail. In fact it was like doing a double act again, but instead of 'You'll bring Mike with you?' it was 'You'll bring Schnorbitz?'

I did wonder if it wasn't all getting a little out of hand, though, when we were invited to a small village just outside Chester to open a fete. There were banners across the street saying in huge letters 'CHESTER WELCOMES SCHNORBITZ' and then underneath, so you could hardly see it, 'and Bernie Winters'. In fact wherever we went we got the red carpet treatment. Even in hotels which normally wouldn't allow a dog on the premises for love nor money, the management would fall over themselves to make her welcome. It would be 'Schnorbitz is coming in today. Make sure the revolving doors are stretched open and she's made to feel at home.' We'd arrive, the doormen would be there to greet her and the manager would appear, just as though royalty had arrived. 'Schnorbitz, of course. How lovely to see you.' Then we'd be shown up to a suite where she'd be given real star treatment. Steak Diane and steak tartare would be delivered on silver platters – it was just a shame she didn't drink champagne – and I could actually take her into dining rooms where the waiters and waitresses would be honoured to have her. The guests loved her as well – so much so that if we were staying over some occasion like New Year's Eve, Schnorbitz would be invited too. 'Do you think she'd come down and join us at our celebration?'

But she never once got big-headed, even when they stopped work to honour her presence at the Rolls-Royce factory at Crewe. I'd just bought a beautiful Silver Spur and they rang me to invite me down. 'You'll bring Schnorbitz to lunch, of course,' they said. The Queen had just visited that factory and they laid out the red carpet for her as you'd expect, but they kept the factory running. When Schnorbitz went down, however, the machines were stopped completely because they were worried that little bits of steel might get into her paws as she walked through. They'd also made her a special cover which they fitted to protect the leather seats at the back of the car. She graciously sat on it so that they could take photos of her.

When I was doing pantomime at Newcastle I'd be travelling up and back for weeks rehearsing my part, but of course the star didn't have to arrive until two days before the show opened. Prince Charles had gone there by train a week earlier and they'd had the stationmaster out with the red carpet and bowler hat to welcome him. When the Theatre Royal contacted the station to let them know when Schnorbitz would be arriving they laid on identical treatment. The carriage stopped exactly where the red carpet had been laid out, the staff were out in their bowler hats and there were newspaper photographers and television cameras there – the local news was full of 'Schnorbitz Arrives at Newcastle'. She was becoming a superstar.

Schnorbitz was even invited to Buckingham Palace, which turned out to be a relief to both Cliff Richard and me. We'd been asked by Anne Shelton to take part in a show on behalf of the Duchess of Kent for British ex-servicemen, to be called *Lest We Forget*. Before the show started we were taken round the stables so that Schnorbitz could meet the beautiful horses, and then given lunch. It was mutton stew, which is neither Cliff's nor my favourite. I started surreptitiously dropping bits of mine into Schnorbitz's bowl and Cliff asked me if it would be all right if he gave her his as well. Luckily she loved it, and it made a significant dent in the tons of food she needs a day.

When I first started out with my new partner, but wasn't doing terribly well in the theatre, Cavendish Woodhouse got in touch with us to see if we would do personal appearances at the openings of their newly refurbished furniture stores. Needless to say we were delighted to accept and, in total contrast to the farce that we were appearing in at the time, we were an absolute hit. The firm had some five hundred stores at that stage, and we were flown to Scotland and Northern Ireland as well as travelling all around England and Wales to visit them all. They only wanted us between eleven and one during the day, so it was perfect – we could still be at the theatre every night. It was wonderful: hundreds and thousands of people would come to see us – well, Schnorbitz mostly – and while I busily signed autographs Schnorbitz would have a huge fuss made of her. Unfortunately some of the younger children would sometimes get a bit over-enthusiastic and touch her and crawl over her and bang her on the head; even though she's got a wonderful nature she'd get fed up with that. Siggi would try to cordon her off but Schnorbitz would hit her with her paw (which is some paw to be hit by – like being clobbered by twelve stone of meat) as if to say 'I want to get out of here' and escape upstairs to the office, refusing to come out again until everyone had gone. But all in all it worked very well and it was a relief to know that people really did like us, despite what was happening in the theatre.

There was, however, one very frightening episode amongst those really rather enjoyable trips around the country. It happened when we went to open a store in Belfast. We were flown out there in a private jet with Cavendish Woodhouse's managing director, and half an hour before we arrived we suddenly heard that an anonymous threat had been made on Schnorbitz's life. I was petrified. When we landed what seemed like hundreds of police and security people were there to meet us and we went to the store under a heavy escort of cars. I don't think I've ever wished that something would finish as much as that visit. Luckily nothing happened and we got safely back on the plane with Schnorbitz none the wiser.

After a few years of working with Schnorbitz I decided to put myself on the spot and see if I could manage a show with just the two of us. I had done well enough in pantomime to be confident about taking top billing again, and I didn't want to end my career without discovering whether I could stand on a stage without Mike or any other support. My agent, Peter Prichard, was quite shocked by my change of heart and said, 'I can't possibly book you as a stand-up. I'd be so embarrassed.'

'*You'd* be embarrassed,' I replied. 'How do you think *I'm* going to feel? After all, I'm the one who'll be out there dying on stage.' Anyway, he finally agreed and I was booked for a twenty-week summer season called *It's Bernie's Crazy House* at Babbacombe, just outside Torquay.

I knew that I could never be as good as Mike and I had been together. We'd had so much talent, particularly after so many years of practice; but I was still determined to have a go. As I have said before, I am not a stand-up comedian who tells jokes so I tried the kind of Max Bygraves approach of telling stories. I also sang Bud Flanagan songs and did a few bits of business with Schnorbitz.

The show was going fairly well until one day I went back after a game of golf to the flat I was renting to find Schnorbitz outside rather than inside the front door. She was quaking and whining and had obviously hurt herself. I realized that she must have mistaken the window in the flat for our patio doors at home and, nudging it open, had stepped outside. Unfortunately, unlike home the flat was on the first floor, and her step outside led to a fall which broke her collar bone. The local vet was marvellous and Schnorbitz recovered perfectly, but in the meantime I had to borrow a Yorkshire terrier to take her place, which somehow wasn't quite the same. Schnorbitz still may not have forgiven me for putting her through all that, but I had to see how I'd be if I was completely on my own. I promise you, Schnorbitz, I won't do it again.

One of the proudest moments was when she won the Pro-Dogs gold medal for the Pet of the Year Award. It was a proper function, held at the Grosvenor Hotel in Willesden, for honoured dogs who had performed courageous acts. The humans wore black suits and evening dress, and all the dogs were served dinner next to their owners at the tables. After the meal there was a fashion show where dogs paraded along wearing the latest in doggie coats, leads and collars. Schnorbitz was fascinated watching the model dogs walk by. Then came the highlight of the evening: the actual awards ceremony. I had to say a few words on her behalf and I broke down, mainly because I've never won anything myself, but we treasure her gold medal very much; it has pride of place on the mantelpiece.

Schnorbitz has been a very lucky dog for me. I always seem to perform better when she's there. I'm not sure why, but I think it's because she gives me confidence. I can look at her and see what she's up to – generally sleeping, completely comfortable being on stage or in front of a camera in a television studio, and it's catching. She was with me for the introduction and end of *It's Bernie* and in the ring for the *Big Top Variety*. She didn't have a huge role in *Make Me Laugh*, a show I made for Tyne Tees which launched new comedians like Bobby Davro and Brian Marshall. They were put on the spot by having to make a particular member of the audience crack up, which wasn't easy because of course that person was determined not to laugh. Schnorbitz did make a brief appearance on the end credits, though. She wasn't with me at all for another programme I made for HTV, *Scribble*, which was more of a straightforward quiz show; maybe that's why it didn't work too well. She was there all the time on Thames Television's *Whose Baby?*, though, and was brilliant, even if she did sleep through most of it.

We made those shows over three years in the mid-eighties and they went down very well. I nearly didn't get that job at all. Leslie Crowther had been presenting it, but when he got the job as presenter of *The Price is Right* he had to give up *Whose Baby?* Schnorbitz and I weren't the immediate choice to replace him, but apparently the producer of *Whose Baby?*, Brian Klein, was also working on *This Is Your Life* when I guested on the programme for Danny La Rue.

I came on with a load of other Water Rats from the showbiz charity organisation and, as they organized the walk-on alphabetically, I was last. Brian was so impressed with the reaction I got from the audience that he mentioned it to Philip Jones and suggested me for *Whose Baby?* Funny how these things happen. Anyway, when Philip approached me with the idea of hosting the show I turned it down, thinking that I wouldn't be very good with children and young babies; but Siggi told me she thought it was a marvellous opportunity and that I should give it a try. I'm pleased I did – I thought it was one of the best game shows I'd done. The only problem with the show was that we were always worried that there weren't enough babies around, so I used to tell my friends to go home and make babies so we could carry on doing the programme.

It was a simple show. We'd have a baby or child on the couch (and the child could be an adult) with the parents hidden away backstage. Then the celebrity panel would have to ask the child questions so that they could guess who the parents were. You've heard the old showbiz adage about never working with animals or children – well, this really was taking the bull by the horns.

One week the guest was Mary Chipperfield from the famous

circus family. Instead of a child she brought along a chimp called Kong dressed in a sailor suit. As soon as he spotted Schnorbitz, who was lying peacefully eating some sausages, he made a beeline for her. He had a good look for any twiddly bits to pull, and then when he realized Schnorbitz was a female he decided to punch her in the stomach instead. I thought World War III was about to break out. Schnorbitz is normally very docile, but there are limits. The whole thing turned into a fiasco, with Schnorbitz trying to bat the chimp across the studio with her paws. Eventually everything calmed down, and we were about to proceed with the show when Kong realized he was thirsty. So he jumped straight on to the panel's desk and seized Nanette Newman's glass of water. We all watched in stunned amazement while he drank the whole thing down in one go. I was very worried that Nanette would be frightened out of her life, but she put out her hand to stroke him, telling him that he was a lovely boy. Another crisis averted.

Mostly, though, Schnorbitz enjoyed herself. When it was her birthday the canteen ladies at Thames Television very kindly made her a huge cake from sausages, in the shape of a cat. Spike Milligan was one of the guests that week. When the cake was brought on as a surprise presentation to Schnorbitz he watched her gobble it up and shouted, 'My cat! I wondered what had happened to it.' He's so good at that type of spontaneous humour.

Schnorbitz had her own contract with the television company and lunched with the rest of us in the executive dining room. The new producer, Maurice Leonard, was most offended when he heard management mutterings threatening to ban her from eating with us. 'But she's an artiste,' he said. 'She can't possibly be banned.' So to wind him up even more we typed out a memo purporting to be from the head of administration. It said: 'Schnorbitz is no longer permitted to eat in the restaurant. If she's seen there again I will be forced to disallow both her and the producer from using these facilities again.' Maurice hit the roof and was about to go and bang his fist on a few desks when we told him it was just a joke.

What with all the animals and the children on the show you could forgive me for getting confused sometimes. Pia Zadora was a guest one week. She had flown in specially on her private plane to be on the show with her new baby. She brought with her a retinue of agents and managers – very much the American way of doing things – but when Schnorbitz and I went to the Hospitality Room to meet her she'd disappeared. One of the managers told me that she had taken the baby for a walk, but for some obscure reason I turned to Maurice and said, 'She's out walking the dog.' Pia wasn't very impressed with me, either, when her baby was brought on stage and put into my arms (I had to answer the panel's questions for her). One look at my face and the baby screamed the place down, nearly wriggled out of my arms and gave me a good soaking. Mum threw me a look of sheer disgust when she came on stage, and I gratefully gave her back her child.

Someone else I seemed to frighten was the small son of the dress designers, the Emanuels. He and his sister were dressed like a dream for the show, and beforehand he was very chatty and happily playing with Schnorbitz. When it came to actually coming on, however, he bawled his eyes out and refused point-blank. Sarah, the hostess, came out with his sister, looking slightly battered from trying to persuade him that he really would enjoy it. He never came on – in fact we're still waiting for him.

There were times, as well, when ambition overtook practicality. The first was when the Three Degrees were guests on the show and there seemed to be hundreds of children sitting on the couch with me. The panel guessed who their mothers were, and when they came on the children had to move to make space for them to sit down. This gave them licence to play. Within seconds they were all over the place, running from one end of the stage to the other and climbing all over the back of the couch. It was lovely watching the cameraman going frantic, trying to keep them all in shot.

Another time the surprise guests were the West Ham football team. That meant eleven players plus reserves and something like thirty children from six weeks old upwards. It was a logistical nightmare, especially as we had to keep them hidden from the panel before the show and then try to keep them quiet backstage. At one stage, when it sounded as though there was a riot going on behind the scenes, Nanette Newman commented that it sounded like a football team. And when they came on it was pretty obvious that it must be.

Siggi and Ray sometimes came to the recordings, and poor old Ray nearly got hauled on to the show on one occasion. He's not the least bit interested in show business and can't bear the idea of being in front of a camera, but when a guest hadn't arrived before we started the show he reluctantly agreed to stand in. He had his make-up put on and was so nervous it was streaked with sweat. He was saved at the last minute, though, when the missing guest turned up. If ever I suggested to Siggi that she might have to come on the show to help out she'd run out of the studio.

I met lots of really interesting and different people through *Whose Baby?* Some, like Vince Hill and Frank Bruno, became good friends. When Vince appeared he brought his son, Athol. The panel successfully guessed who his father was and when Vince came on I had to ask how Athol got his name as it's so unusual. He explained that he and his wife had tried for years to have a baby, with no joy, and had just started adoption proceedings when they discovered she was pregnant. Their son was conceived one weekend away in a pub called the Athol Arms. Then there was big Frank Bruno. He arrived with his children and his manager Terry Lawless, who made a bet with Frank that he wouldn't be able to stroke Schnorbitz. It's unbelievable, but the man who would get in a ring with Mike Tyson is frightened of dogs. I was just as scared when I took his hand to help him touch Schnorbitz in case he turned round and gave me a left hook. But he managed to stroke her, and luckily he won the bet.

And I was honoured to meet people like Sir Georg Solti, ex-Prime Minister James Callaghan with his entourage of grandchildren and great-grandchildren, and Denis Healey. When the last of these was due to appear, Philip Jones sent me a message that I should make a special effort to ask a political question. I'm not very good at that kind of thing, and when it came to it I dried. The only thing I could think of asking him was, 'When you trim your eyebrows do your trousers fall down?' If Mr Healey hadn't laughed I think I might have been sacked. The late Eamonn Andrews was very kind about me on *Whose Baby?* He had devised the programme and even presented one series, but I discovered later that he thought I'd been the best host the show ever had – well, apart from Schnorbitz of course.

Of the three Schnorbitzes each one has been as lovely as the last, and it's true what they say – a man's best friend is his dog. Best showbiz partner as well.

10

FLANAGAN AND ALLEN

THERE was a night in 1980 which could have ended in a minor disaster but in fact became one of the best nights of my life. I'd been asked with Schnorbitz to present an award at the annual *TV Times* Awards ceremony. It was for female television personality of the year and I was to give it to Barbara Woodhouse, who was so incredible at training dogs. Now there's only one thing that sends Schnorbitz demented and that's the sound of balloons bursting. So I started to worry when I saw the room was filled with them. All was going swimmingly, however, until Barbara came on stage to receive her trophy and BANG, a balloon burst. Before I knew what was happening, the normally passive Schnorbitz bolted to the back of the stage. You'd think it would be the perfect situation – here was a terrified dog and here was the best animal trainer anyone had ever heard of. I just panicked, but Barbara instantly took control. 'Don't worry, I'll handle this,' she said as she went off after Schnorbitz. 'Sit-t-t-t!' she commanded to a quaking mass of St Bernard. Ordinarily this would be enough to pull any demented animal to its senses. Not so Schnorbitz; when Barbara tried to get her to sit upright, she was dealing with a ton of reluctant dog who wasn't about to do anything other than cower and shake. Of course the audience thought it was hysterical, but I felt dreadful and apologised profusely to Barbara, who luckily took it in good heart. I went back to my table half wishing that the ground would swallow me and Schnorbitz up.

After the ceremony was over I met up with an old friend, Sid Collins, who was the programme controller at Yorkshire Television. He told me he was writing a musical about the life of Bud Flanagan and asked me whether I'd be interested in playing the lead role. In fact, he said, he was writing it with me in mind. I couldn't believe it. It was the best offer I'd had since going solo, and it was quite unexpectedly being dropped in my lap. Naturally I said I'd be delighted, if he really thought I was capable of doing it.

The whole episode seemed fated to happen, and it was incredible when it did. Right from my childhood, Bud Flanagan had played an important part in my life. During the war and just afterwards my parents, like many others, were regulars at the variety concerts held at the Moss Empire theatres and they took us kids with them. One of the highlights was to see comedy duos like Flanagan and Allen. Of course Mike and I didn't know then that we'd also end up doing a double act, but maybe somewhere in the back of our minds they sowed the seeds for what would happen to us. The unusual thing was that my father, Mougie, got to know them. They were very keen on racing and Royal Ascot was a big event for them. Mougie would always be there as well and over the years, as Mike and I made our start in show business, he'd often talk horses with Bud and tell him about us and what we were up to. Mougie would come home and say, 'I saw Bud Flanagan today and he said that you've got to go on and keep trying, keep at it all the time.' And he'd make us rehearse.

Then years later, after Siggi and I had definitely decided to get married and when Mike and I were more successful, I met Bud for the first time. Siggi was dancing in a show called *These Foolish Kings* at the Victoria Palace in London with the Crazy Gang, and whenever I wasn't working I'd go and wait for her outside the stage door. Sometimes Bud would come out before

Siggi and would be absolutely charming. He'd ask after my dad and how Mike and I were doing with our act, and was always really encouraging. When I could I'd watch the show from the side of the stage. He was working on his own by this time; I realized the man was an absolute genius and became a real fan.

If it's not too presumptuous, there have been a lot of similarities in our lives as well. He was Jewish too and was born almost a stone's throw from Islington, in the East End. He ran away to America when he was about fourteen and I went off to sea in the merchant navy at seventeen. We both did double acts, we both married dancers and we both finished up working on our own. Even more coincidentally, as I mentioned earlier, when I arrived in Sydney with the merchant navy Bud's son Buddy, who was disc jockeying there, put me in touch with an upcoming talent competition at which I won first prize. It was £1 – a hell of a lot of money in those days – and it bought us all a very good night out.

The coincidences were destined to carry on. In the sixties Mike and I took part in a show at the Empire Theatre in Liverpool for the late Richard Armitage, with Russ Abbot and the Springfields. We were asked to sing 'Underneath the Arches', and at every performance we stopped the show with it – it became the hit of the evening. I hadn't realized the power that Flanagan and Allen had and the magic of their music. A few years later our agent Joe Collins called us down to his office and said that Chesney Allen, who by this time had also become an agent, had been on the phone to suggest that we get together and create a show in which Mike and I would play Flanagan and Allen. Rather naïvely, we thought we were too hip for that at the time.

So when Sid Collins told me about his musical it seemed like the most natural thing in the world, as well as being a tremendous honour. Within a year ATV contacted my agent to ask if I'd play Bud in Sid's *Bud 'n' Ches*, with Leslie Crowther playing Chesney Allen. Naturally we accepted. It was the first time in my life that I'd actually gone to a television studio for a whole five weeks to rehearse. John Schofield was the producer and Nigel Lythgoe the director, choreographer – and boy, did we work hard for them. We rehearsed songs with Jack Parnell and his orchestra, and did dozens of classes working out with the dancers – that was very pleasant; the girls were lovely and I enjoyed that a lot. The script was huge, a big book with lots of songs and lots of choreographic work to learn. But Leslie has a brilliant brain and knew virtually the whole thing by the end of the first day of rehearsals.

We rehearsed and taped every day, and as it was the first television drama I'd been in I was dying to see the rushes. John Schofield forbade it, however, except on one occasion. It was the day I had sung 'Any Umbrellas?' on my own. The studio was blacked out and I was standing on the top of a ladder wearing a big fur coat. The camera was on a crane, high up with me, and Jack Parnell was playing the music. Then the strangest thing happened. Up there, completely alone in the darkness, I really felt as though I was with Bud, singing beside him. The emotion of the moment got to me and I started to cry during the song. I managed to get to the end and then apologised to John and told him I'd do it again straightaway, this time without the tears. He told me not to worry since we were finished for the day, and got the floor manager to put a monitor near me so that I could see it. It was the first time I was going to be allowed to watch what I'd done, and I thought it was to teach me a lesson because I'd messed it up so badly. When it was over John's voice came back at me over the tannoy system, and to my utter relief he told me it was marvellous.

I never actually saw the whole thing until it went out on air a few weeks later, so I really didn't know what to expect. The moment it finished the phone didn't stop ringing for five hours. The world and its brother were calling me – Eric Morecambe, Jimmy Tarbuck, Bob Monkhouse, agents, friends, half the world of showbiz. Leslie was getting the same number of calls at his end, but eventually we managed to get through to each other. Apparently television company switchboards around the country were jammed as well, by callers offering their congratulations and telling them what a wonderful show it was.

I was up in heaven, and began to think what a wonderful idea it would be to make it a stage musical and take the show on the road. I approached the theatre impresario Bill Kenwright with the idea. He agreed, and so Leslie and I started rehearsing again. What we didn't know, though, was that Roy Hudd was at that very moment opening in *Underneath the Arches*, another musical about Flanagan and Allen. Apparently after we recorded *Bud 'n' Ches* for ATV at Elstree during the day, our Crazy Gang cast had been going down to Chichester at night to rehearse for *Underneath the Arches*, so we should have known there was another production. But Bill decided to go ahead with us anyway.

I went along to see Roy's show at Chichester, and I was so impressed that I went straight backstage to congratulate him and his co-star, Christopher Timothy. We were very unlucky with the timing of our production. Soon afterwards, when Bernard Delfont needed a show quickly to play at the Prince of Wales Theatre in London, ours still wasn't up and running so he put in *Underneath the Arches*. Even so, we persisted with *Bud 'n' Ches* and took it around the provinces. At first we did very well. We sold out in Eastbourne and Brighton but then, as we went further north, the houses started to thin out. We went to Wilmslow, just outside Manchester, and emptied the place. Same thing at the King's Theatre in Glasgow. I remember Jimmy Logan coming to see us backstage after one of the performances and telling us that he loved the show but that we'd made a real mistake calling it *Bud 'n' Ches* – people would think we were Chas 'n' Dave. He thought that if we changed the name to *Flanagan and Allen* we'd go down a storm. I don't know how true that was, but I know it was a smashing show and that Leslie and I loved doing it.

Bill Kenwright loved it as well. Although he was losing money he kept it going. He was fantastic. He even brought his family when we played the Empire in Liverpool and told us that even if the houses weren't that good it was still the best production he'd ever put on. Years later I did the television programme *Search for a Star* with him. It was taped in a packed theatre, and as we sat up in the box as part of the panel I said, 'You see, Bill? Eventually we've found an audience.' He's a wonderful man and if ever I get real box office pulling power I promise, Bill, I'll do a show for you for nothing.

Leslie was fantastic, too. You could never be depressed with him – he wouldn't let you. Even when there was just Bill and his family sitting out in the audience at a matinee, he'd take a peek and tell you that the place was buzzing. And he'd always be at the side of the stage, dropping his trousers or pulling ridiculous faces to make you laugh. We had a funny time one Saturday afternoon. When we started the show there was a total of fifteen people in the stalls. Then, during the interval, the Lord Mayor's parade passed by the theatre and four of them left. We claim now that instead of doing the second act, we played them at football and lost three-nil. I've worked with Leslie now for many years on and off and he's always been marvellous to be with, even though he's had enough problems in his own life. He's also one of the most honourable people I've met. His word is his bond. We were invited one year to take part in a Royal Command Performance as Flanagan and Allen, but he'd already agreed to open a fete in Chippenham and wouldn't break his word to do the Royal Command instead.

Well before that, though, while we were still touring with *Bud 'n' Ches*, we did appear at the Royal Command Performance as Flanagan and Allen. We did very well, too – so well that the theatre producer, Richard Mills, came over to us at the party afterwards and asked us if we'd take over from Roy Hudd and Christopher Timothy at the Prince of Wales as their run was coming to an end after fifteen months. I said yes instantly, because you can't keep me away from anything in the West End or from working with Leslie. It so happens, too, that the Prince of Wales is a theatre I love. It holds great memories for me, because when I was a child I used to go and watch one of the greatest comedians I've ever seen in my life, Sid Fields. I'd get a three-bob ticket called a rover, or a shilling one, and watch him perform as often as I could – I loved him. So for me to star there as Bud Flanagan in the Number One dressing room, which Sid Fields would have used, was to me – well, you couldn't give me anything better.

While we rehearsed *Underneath the Arches* we changed it a little, put in extra songs and tried to make it a bit more dramatic. It was a comedy, unlike *Bud 'n' Ches* which was more the straightforward story of Bud's life. When the first night came I was more nervous than I'd ever been on stage before. But we needn't have worried. Leslie and I trotted on, and there in the audience were lots of our friends, like Ronnie Barker, Frankie Vaughan, Danny La Rue, Barbara Windsor and Lionel Blair. Cavendish Woodhouse had done me a huge favour and recarpeted Number One dressing room, and we had a marvellous party after the show to celebrate our first night. Normally when a show is over you don't see me for dust – I'm out of the theatre before anyone. But in that place they couldn't get rid of me. I used to stay in the dressing room till one or two in the morning to have a drink and a chat with people who popped round to see me starring in the West End, for the very first time on my own. It was wonderful, and I loved every minute of it. Unfortunately we were only in there for fourteen weeks; the show had by then been on for eighteen months and had run its course. It was sad when it closed, but it's an unfortunate fact of life that all shows eventually come to an end.

The last night was incredible. Most nights I got a standing ovation, but this time from the moment the curtain went up until the moment it came down again was a revelation – I've never known anything like it. People just didn't stop cheering. It was a magical time in the theatre, one that I'm sure I won't have again.

Since then Bud has become a large part of my life. Although I'm not playing him on stage any more I'm often asked to sing his songs at different events, either on my own or with Leslie for the Bud Flanagan Leukaemia Fund. One time was at Windsor where the Duke of Edinburgh was guest of honour. The show was for the Grand Order of Water Rats and run by David Kaye. I felt as though I was getting to know the Duke quite well by then and was asked to present him with a gold straw hat as the finale after David presented the cheque. When he and the Duke of Edinburgh get together they do a kind of double act; with David being so small and the Duke towering elegantly above him, they look marvellous. This night David started his speech: 'I'm happy to present you with a cheque for £25,000, Your Royal Highness. This is such a marvellous moment for me.'

'Oh really? Yes,' said the Duke.

David replied 'Yes, it is. I mean the honour and the thrill of presenting you with a cheque for £25,000 is simply remarkable.'

The Duke thanked him.

David carried on: 'Yes, I mean moments like this don't come every day, you know, Your Royal Highness. To give you this cheque for £25,000 . . . well . . . it's very difficult for me to do.'

Finally the Duke came back: 'And it's getting more and more difficult for me to receive it.' That got a very big laugh.

Then I presented him with the gold hat and we stood around chatting until his equerry told him it was time to leave. At which point Su Pollard piped up, 'Look here, I've only got a Vauxhall Viva, but if you like I'll give you a lift.'

The Duke replied, 'Well, that's very kind of you, my dear, but I only live around the corner. I think I'll walk.'

It's quite incredible to think that Bud Flanagan still holds such a strong place in so many hearts. I've been singing his songs for almost ten years now, but I'd never have thought when we first started rehearsing *Bud 'n' Ches* all that time ago that people would still be asking me to put on the old fur coat and hat and perform 'Strolling' or 'Underneath the Arches'. It's phenomenal, and I'm delighted to be a part of it. When leukaemia finally took Bud's life I sent a wreath to his funeral. His widow very kindly wrote to me to say how much I now reminded her of her husband. That's such an honour for me. I still have the letter, and I treasure both it and the opportunity to play Bud whenever possible.

11

GOOD TIMES, GOOD FRIENDS

THE most wonderful thing I've found about show business is the people you meet, from royalty to the most successful businessmen and sportsmen as well as some of the world's top entertainers. I am still over-awed by them all, and it's a privilege to be able to count some of them amongst my friends. Sometimes when I think about having shaken hands with the Queen I have to pinch myself. It's a long way from the kid who ran round the backstreets of Tottenham without shoes. But Mum was right with her prophecies. She said that one day we'd live in a castle, and I did in a way. By the seventies I had a beautiful house in Cockfosters, Hertfordshire, and drove a series of Roll-Royce cars.

My best friends who aren't connected with show business are all very successful in business and I've shared with them the kind of high life I imagined only existed in *Dynasty* or *Dallas*. Lou Manzie, David Mason and Ray Stevens are my kind of people: they work hard and play hard, and we have had some incredible times together. Ray Stevens, an industrialist, has become a very good friend in the last few years. He holds an annual ball for two to three hundred people at his home in the country, and no expense is spared. I call him Mr Dom Pérignon. In 1990 he started the day at Newmarket Races, where he had an enormous marquee at the finishing post. He'd had everyone driven there in limousines, as the wine was flowing freely from 11.30 a.m. It was a gloriously hot day in July and Jimmy Tarbuck and I were sitting under a sun umbrella drinking it all in. Suitably relaxed, we grabbed the umbrella and provided everybody with a duet of 'Strolling', causing complete havoc amongst the other racegoers. Given the amount we drank at Newmarket, I wondered whether we'd last into the evening's festivities. I knew I had to because I was MC-ing the entertainment, so after the drive back to Ray's house I had a jacuzzi and a nap. Jimmy had a swim and a sauna and was as bright as a button when he did a spot of entertaining later on. It was a brilliant night. Ray had laid on cabaret from Wayne Dobson and the RAF band, but as it approached 2.30 a.m. I announced that the band was shutting up shop. I wanted to get down to the Dom Pérignon, lobster and caviar that I'd been missing out on all evening, but as I thanked everyone for coming to the party Ray ran up to me frantically to say I couldn't possibly send everyone home yet as he had planned breakfast for 5 a.m. So Jimmy and I really let them have it, singing all the old rock and roll favourites and jiving round the stage.

Ray really knows how to enjoy his money and is generous to a fault. Sometimes he's rung me in the morning and asked if I fancy lunch in Germany or Monte Carlo. The first time he took me on his Lear jet I made a complete idiot of myself. We went to Stuttgart, and as soon as I was served with coffee up in the air I pulled the table out of its sockets and threw the drink all over myself. I spent the rest of the journey half naked while my trousers dried.

I nearly managed to blow it again on a trip with some other friends. I'd always dreamt of a sailing holiday in the lap of luxury and they'd invited us to join them. The yacht was enormous with a captain, a cook and four crew, and it was wonderful – we enjoyed sunbathing, water skiing and swimming off the boat, and there was a motor launch. We sailed from

Dubrovnik along the coast to some beautiful islands off Yugoslavia, and then on to Venice. I've never particularly wanted to go there, but sailing along the Grand Canal and mooring at St Mark's Square was quite an experience. We had dinner that night at the famous Cipriani Hotel, and when I ordered veal and my usual tomato ketchup my friends were absolutely appalled: 'We bring you to the top hotel and you embarrass us by asking for tomato sauce.' Luckily I was saved by the head waiter recognizing me. He'd worked in England and seen me on television, so he was all over me. 'Eh! I see you on television wiz zee dog Schnorboatz!' After I'd signed several autographs I was redeemed. My friend had ordered prawns, which disagreed with him, so I told him he should have had tomato sauce with them and he'd have been all right. Unfortunately I had to miss the last trip around the Greek islands due to ill health.

Another holiday took Siggi and me to Las Vegas. America to me has always meant movies, Disneyland, magic and Hollywood. We checked in at the incredible Caesar's Palace, where Siggi made straight for the slot machines. I had a wander round the hotel and noticed lots of canopied barrows laden with every type of food you can imagine and tables straining under the weight of hundreds of bottles of booze by the pool. Naturally I assumed this was a reception for the hotel guests but as I went to go through the door two enormous heavies stopped me to ask if I was with the convention. I didn't know what they were talking about, but it all looked too good to miss and so I said, 'Oh yes. I'm from London' and they ushered me in. I was eating everything in sight – crayfish, lobster, hamburgers and helped myself to an armful of bourbon and Coke. It turned out it was a lawyers' convention but I managed to side-step the 'Are you a lawyer?' questions from everybody and just said, 'I'm from England.' Fortunately they all had a story to tell about when they had visited London, so I ended up having a great time with them and was the last to leave. After that I decided Caesar's

Palace really wasn't that bad.

Usually people only go there for two days, but we were booked in for twelve so that we could travel around to various places like Lake Mead. I don't gamble much – just the odd poker game for three dollars maximum – but Siggi loves it and would stay up all night while I'd sit in the bar or go to the room and watch TV. One night I was at the bar when an English guy came up to me and said 'Hello! remember me?' I vaguely recognised him as an English reporter I'd met and he invited me to dinner at Caesar's Room, the best restaurant in the hotel. It was splendidly decorated, and the waitresses were dressed in togas with big vases on their heads. The reporter told me we'd have to come up with a good story about me that he could send back to his paper, so that he could claim the dinner on expenses – something like 'Bernie Winters signs $100,000 contract to appear at the Palace'. Then he asked me if I knew Englebert Humperdinck.

Well, of course I had met him, though he was hardly an old friend. But I'd got carried away by this time and said, 'Eng? Sure I know him. Great guy' – not realizing that he was sitting right behind me. So of course this fellow, who had been trying to get an introduction to Englebert for months, pointed at him and said, 'Well, he's only over there – go and say "hello".'

My bluff was called and I had to try to double back: 'Well, he's with a lot of people. I don't want to bother him. I mean I *know* him, but he's not my dearest friend. When I was doing *Big Night Out* from Blackpool he was appearing at the ABC Theatre and he used to come and watch us play football . . . but that's a good few years ago now and he probably won't remember me.' But the reporter persisted, so I walked over to Englebert's table drowning in my own ego and feeling well and truly sunk. I could hear my voice crack as I managed a 'Hello, Engle', expecting to be hauled away by some big bodyguards. I couldn't believe how he reacted.

He jumped up and threw his arms around me. 'Hello, Bernie!'

he said, really pleased to see me. 'What are you doing here?' I explained I was with the reporter and he said, 'After dinner you must bring your wife to see the show at the MGM Grand. I'll send my limo for you.' Caesar's Palace is only across the road from the MGM Grand but he insisted. 'No, I'm sending you the limo, and after the show you'll come up to my room.'

I was absolutely flabbergasted and at eleven o'clock a message was relayed around the hotel 'Paging Mr Winters. Mr Humperdinck's limousine is outside the main lobby for you.' We got into his beautiful white Cadillac, and of course as soon as we had sat down we arrived at the MGM Grand. His dressing room was an enormously vast suite with a bar containing every drink you had ever heard of, and enough tureens and salvers of food for dozens of people. Englebert told me to come and eat there every night at about the same time, as the food and drink were complimentary. He seemed genuinely delighted to see us, and the next night invited us to his house for dinner.

His house was a mansion with guards at the gate and he showed me a bedroom where a remote control operated a television which appeared as if from nowhere up out of the floor. 'Dino likes to use this. I let him stay here when he's playing in town.' Of course he was talking about Dean Martin and I was even more over-awed. His kindness was overwhelming. He organized free tables for us every night for all the shows at the Flamingo, Caesar's Palace and the Desert Inn. I can never thank him enough for those incredible days out there. Engle, bless you.

Some years before, when I was still with Mike, Siggi and I had gone to Las Vegas for the first time. Michael Grade was our agent then and had told a friend of his, who was the entertainments director of the Flamingo Hotel, that we were coming. It certainly meant star treatment, and before long Des O'Connor joined us out there. Everything had been arranged for us. We were booked into shows and restaurants and, even though I knew my heart would sink when I was given the bill to sign, I'd calm myself down by thinking it was a once-in-a-lifetime experience. Unlike me, Des was a star in America as well. His British television shows had been broadcast out there, so he had to stand and take a bow wherever we went. When he waved I'd get hold of his hands and make a big show of filing his nails, but he forgave my little joke.

One of the shows we saw starred the comedian Don Rickles, who is my hero. His technique was to discover who in the audience was famous and then take the mickey out of them. So when he found out about Des he said, 'We have some lousy English singer here with us tonight. He's called Des O'Connor and I know he's a top star in England because he's called me twenty times to tell me so.' Des took it in good heart – after all, he'd had enough practice with the stick he used to get from Morecambe and Wise. I was very honoured after the show to be taken with Des to meet Don, and delighted to find my intuition correct – he was a lovely man. We had a wonderful holiday there, but my heart was in my boots when it came to paying the bill. So I couldn't believe it when all they wanted me to pay for was our laundry. Thank you, Michael Grade and the Flamingo Hotel, and if there is ever anything I can do to pay you back . . . .

Siggi and I spend most of our holidays in Spain, where we have a small apartment. The village we stay in is a very relaxed place, where you can wander around in shorts or jeans and enjoy either a five-star kind of life relatively cheaply or go into tapas bars even more cheaply and have good food and drink and good fun nights. We always meet up with lots of friends in Spain. One of them is Eddie Avis, the ex-British light heavyweight and Commonwealth boxing champion and part owner of one of my favourite restaurants there. He is one of the characters in the village and calls me Bungy. His restaurant is the meeting place for everybody. You arrive with a few friends and end up on a table for twenty when people like Shirley Bassey or Freddie Starr turn up. Siggi and I asked Eddie to lay on a special meal for us a few years ago for our thirtieth wedding anniversary. Jimmy Tarbuck, Bruce Forsyth, Jess Conrad and Des O'Connor were there and it was a lovely, lovely evening. Des crowned it all by having a special 'long service' medal specially made for us.

One year while we were there Frank Bruno was boxing at the bullring. Eddie had a lot of tickets and we arranged to meet at the restaurant and then go on to the fight. The MC spotted Jimmy Tarbuck, Kenny Lynch and me in the front row and called us up into the ring. I didn't want to go but Jimmy dragged me up, took the mike and said how fantastic it was to be there, how we were really looking forward to seeing Frank fight and that I wanted to sing a song for everybody. I could have killed him. He left me there holding the mike, trying to sing a song with no music and feeling really embarrassed – until someone in the audience shouted, 'If you don't shut up I'll come up there and knock you out in a minute!' I got out pretty quickly.

Things can get very drunken and silly at this particular restaurant. One night I was there with Lionel Blair and Peter Stringfellow, the nightclub owner. I was wearing my favourite pink silk shirt with fancy collar and cuffs when Eddie took a liking to it. Lionel and Peter got into action, stripping it off me and dressing me in a tablecloth. Then they laid me out on a table and began operating on me, calling for knives, scalpels, raspberries and profiteroles.

Ray Stevens has a beautiful villa nearby and is an incredible host. When he invites you out to dinner you meet at the villa for champagne and caviar, then go off to a restaurant. The first time Siggi and I went I assumed that that was dinner – but he said, 'No, no. This is just a snack' and proceeded to throw away what we hadn't drunk 'so the children don't get to it'! The villa is enormous, with a special barbecue room and eating area built on to the side, and in 1990 he threw a party there for Kevin Keegan, Jimmy Tarbuck, Ian St John, Cilla Black, Lionel Blair and us. He'd brought in several cases of a particular Spanish wine that Jimmy adores. I don't remember the name but it sounds like Vidal Sassoon, and that night it flowed non-stop as we sang and danced and played the piano. The party didn't finish till 7 a.m. and we were due on the golf course that morning.

Another friend, Lou Manzie, also enjoys Spain. He owns a string of nightclubs and always stays at the best hotel down there. A typical day with Lou starts with a Dom Pérignon breakfast by the pool and then some gentle sun-bathing; a caviar, smoked salmon or lobster lunch with more champagne is followed by some chilled wine by the pool in the afternoon; after a siesta it's out at night with twenty-odd friends to a restaurant and then on to a bar owned by an enormous Texan who provides his own cabaret of country and western songs. I got up one night to sing 'Strolling' and was so legless I couldn't remember the words. It's a hard life! Lou is a lovely man – a complete lunatic.

Then there's the playboy Robert Windsor, famous for going out with Koo Stark. I've been to four of his weddings so far, but unfortunately he has now taken up residence in Miami. No doubt he is causing complete havoc over there, too. He used to live in Totteridge Lane, a kind of millionaires' row in north London, where he had a vast pink house with one of the largest private collections of exotic birds. At one stage he became the snooker player Cliff Thorburn's manager and one night threw a party for him to celebrate Cliff's birthday and his becoming world champion. It was a great night. James Coburn was there with Lindsay de Paul, Robert Powell, Jimmy Tarbuck and Des O'Connor. When we got to the point where we had all drunk too much but were very happy Des and a pal challenged Cliff and me to a foursome at the snooker table. Cliff gave them a 75-point head start and the first shot of the game was mine. I immediately potted the white ball, so now we were 79 down. Fortunately Des missed his shot, and when Cliff went to the table he cleared it. It was incredible to see, and Cliff and I ended up winning a tenner each.

Robert was also responsible for introducing me to golf – I had always thought the game was boring, preferring football. My first time out was in a pro-celebrity charity match that Robert holds every year to raise money to buy wheelchairs for disabled children. As I stood at the first tee a helicopter landed on my left. My first ball hit it. My partner was the South African golfer Hugh Biaocchi, who fortunately did a lot better than I did and tried to teach me how to play.

I became a golfing addict quite quickly and love taking part in charity events wherever they are. Jimmy Tarbuck's one in Portugal is always great fun, and in 1990 one that Lou Manzie sponsored in Spain became a very drunken occasion. In fact we were so hung-over by the time we played that Lou lost. When it came to presenting the prize to the winner he said, 'I suppose it's just as well. It would have been difficult to give it to myself.' I was very honoured one year to be made captain of the Variety Golfing Club. Henry Cooper was chairman and insisted I take on the captaincy. I was absolutely delighted. It's quite a busy job: you attend all the golf matches, make speeches and present prizes. It is a very well-supported charity and I am in the *Guinness Book of Records* for having raised £200,000 in one day for a game held at Kingsbury Golf Club which was sponsored by Gatwick Airport. Russ Abbot, Petula Clark and Frank Carson did the cabaret after the tournament, and when the Gatwick Airport representative gave me the cheque I said, 'Thank you so much. The wife and I really appreciate it.'

Henry Cooper has been a good friend of mine from way back in the days when we were both teenagers. Mike and I used to frequent a café in Gerrard Street called Peter Mario's which was a meeting place for up-and-coming showbiz personalities. Mario had a daughter called Albina, whom Henry was busily courting. They are still happily married.

I've also met some other good friends through the business. People like the late Matt Monro, Bob Monkhouse, the late

Tommy Cooper, Jimmy Tarbuck and Des O'Connor. I knew Bob for many years through his shows *Celebrity Squares* and *The Golden Shot*, and he frequently guested on Mike's and my shows as a comic or in sketches. It's only in the last few years, though, that we have become really close. It started when Siggi and I were on holiday one year in Barbados. As we wandered down the beach one day we bumped into Jackie Monkhouse. She pointed us towards Bob, who was almost invisible – hiding under a yucca tree and covered from head to foot, with a big naval cap on, to protect him from the sun. He was delighted to see us and invited us for dinner at Baggiwinkle, the bungalow he was renting. It was a splendid place – all very posh with white marble tables and floors and an immaculately dressed butler. Bob is very organized and had a radio and video recorder all set up with videos of plays and movies to watch.

When we sat down to eat at the enormous dining table we were terribly impressed by the service. The moment we laid down our spoons after the first course the butler appeared to collect the plates. It happened the same way every time we finished a dish. I couldn't figure out how he knew precisely when to come in and wondered whether he was peeking through the keyhole. Then, when the coffee arrived right on the nose, Jackie revealed that there was a button on the floor by her feet which she could press to call him.

Tommy Cooper was a good friend too, and I miss him very much. We went right back to the early days, playing in the Soho gangster club the Blue Lagoon and working the markets together. With his big feet he was tall and gangly even then, but he made everybody laugh. He was probably one of the few genuine eccentrics I have met and would provide marvellous entertainment at parties. Tommy had this quirk of bringing his own drink with him and sitting all night with it in a carrier bag between his feet. I was the only other person allowed a swig.

I always remember when he was making a special for Thames Television. The script was written and rehearsed, the artistes booked and the show ready to record. There was a supper break at five o'clock, and Tommy disappeared to the pub next door to have a drink. The audience started to arrive at seven and Tommy was due in make-up at seven-thirty, but he wasn't there. A frantic search party made for the pub, only to discover that he'd got into a cab and driven off to no one knew where. That was the end of the show that night. The producer, the director and everybody at Thames was absolutely furious with him, vowing never to book him again. They did, of course – he was so talented.

I was watching him on *Live from Her Majesty's* the night that he collapsed and died on stage. Eric Sykes told me later at the funeral that Tommy had phoned him that day in a bit of a panic, worried that he had no finish to his act. Eric had replied that he was sure Tommy would think of something. Other than that, no one had a clue that there was anything wrong with him. I was booked for the show the following week, and walking on to the stage that night was one of the hardest things I have ever done. The air seemed so thick with memories of Tommy.

Matt Monro was another dear friend whom sadly we lost too early. We met up when he, Mike and I played the same summer revue season in Weymouth; he and I hit it off instantly – as did our wives, who are both German. We'd play cards all night, or snooker in the holiday camp over the road for a shilling a corner. I ended up owing him £150,000, which he never got. Every time he appeared at the Talk of the Town we were always invited, and he was an excellent host. After the show one night he said, 'You must come backstage I want you to meet someone.' I couldn't believe it when I walked in and there was Tony Bennett. We had a marvellous night together and had to carry Siggi out of the dressing room at four-thirty in the morning drunk as a lord.

Tom Jones was always fun to be with as well. After the Royal Command Performance a couple of years ago Cannon and Ball, Tony Newley, Tom and I had a drink in Tom's dressing room.

I asked him if he was going on to the nightclub Tramp, where I was due to meet up with Lionel Blair, but Tom was going to a big party at the Mayfair Hotel which was being thrown by all the showbiz agents and invited me along too. I'd arranged to meet up with Lionel's daughter Lucy, who was a dancer in the show, to give her a lift to Tramp, but when I looked for her she'd already gone. Lou Manzie and his wife Marion were there that night, so he took us to the nightclub in his very over-the-top long wheelbase Rolls-Royce with spoilers, a TV, bar and chauffeur. When we got to the club Lionel was absolutely furious, and it got even worse when I told him that in fact we weren't staying but were going on to the Mayfair. He doesn't believe to this day that I waited for Lucy, and still has a go at me about it. The party at the Mayfair was fabulous. Tom had his bodyguards all around him and was ordering more and more champagne: 'They're paying paying for it, boyo, so get stuck in.'

Peter Stringfellow is another inveterate partygoer. We go back many years to when Mike and I used to play his northern clubs: the Rockerfella in Leeds and the Millionaire's Club in Manchester. After our act we'd stay up all night playing cards and became good friends. I've spent a lot of time at Stringfellow's and he's always made me feel welcome, with a complimentary bottle of champagne on my table. When he came to my birthday party a few years ago he brought several bottles of Dom Pérignon, two Stringfellow bunny girls complete with tutus, and his pink-haired girlfriend Frisbee. When the party was finally over Peter fell asleep with Schnorbitz on the living-room floor, and I have a photograph of the two of them with their arms around each other to prove it.

Then there are the megastars like Cary Grant and David Niven whom I met in the late sixties. Mike and I were appearing at the Bristol Hippodrome, completely unaware that Cary Grant was in the audience. I was so overwhelmed when the stage doorman came to our dressing room after the show and asked me if we would see Cary Grant. As if we would have said no. It was lovely to meet him and he was very complimentary about our act. He stayed drinking with us until 3 a.m. and invited me to stay with him at his home in Los Angeles. I didn't have the nerve to go, unfortunately. I wish I had. Then we met up with him again a few years later at a variety club in Leeds, where he and David Niven were guests of honour. Cary was as friendly as ever. During dinner with Eric Morecambe I asked him if he could possibly introduce me to David Niven as I had been a fan of his for years. Later on a pair of hands covered my eyes and a voice behind me said, 'It's Bernie Winters. Oh, my God, what a thrill – my favourite, favourite comedian.'

I said, 'Eric, are you mucking about again? Will you stop this? And if that's David Niven can't you see I'm having dinner with my friend Eric Morecambe and we are very busy – we can't possibly sign autographs now.' Lo and behold, it really was David Niven, and we cuddled and kissed each other. What an unforgettable night.

I've also been honoured to meet members of the royal family over the past years. In 1990, when I took part in the march past for the Queen Mother's ninetieth birthday, I found the occasion so moving I couldn't help crying. Later on, after the Royal Gala, I was presented to the Queen Mother, the Queen, Prince Philip and Princess Margaret, who asked me if I had enjoyed the march past. I told her that I'd found it very emotional, and she said she had noticed that I had been crying.

The last time I saw Princess Anne was at the White City dog track for a charity event in aid of the Red Cross. I was having a fit of depression about work at the time, as all comedians get, and when the Princess Royal asked me how I was I told her, 'Not too good.' Then she asked me if I was doing much work and I replied, 'Not really', so she patted me on the back and said, 'Well, I hope you back a few winners tonight, then.'

Showbiz has also helped me to realize other dreams that I

have had, like owning a Rolls-Royce, but I have not necessarily been very lucky with them. When Mike and I first appeared at the Palladium I enthusiastically invited a car dealer to bring a Rolls-Royce to the theatre. It was beautiful and I couldn't resist it, so I signed up to pay £7000 for it. The next day I had the car looked over by my local Rolls-Royce agent, who asked about its history. The dealer told me that none existed for that particular car, and when I contacted the Rolls-Royce company I found out why. The car had been written off in an accident and the chassis was in a real mess. I decided to make the best of it, though, as the dealer wouldn't take it back, and took it through a car wash. It came through the other end looking as though it had been rubbed down with steel wool. My penny-pinching attempt to have it resprayed also went wrong, and the car reappeared with several shades of blue paint over it. That wasn't the end of the misery: the hydraulics went, which meant that whenever I touched the doors I got an electric shock.

Finally I managed to get someone to take it off my hands in part exchange for a Mulliner Park Ward that I'd spotted in a showroom window. It was a special edition Rolls – only twelve were ever made, and this one looked perfect. I had to have it, and agreed to pay £8000 on top of what they were offering for my blue mistake. It wasn't long before I realized that this one had problems, too: it was a convertible, but the hood was so badly sealed that whenever it rained I got drenched. Every time I had it repaired it just seemed to get worse.

Luckily it was a sunny day when I drove Siggi down to Bournemouth in it, so the hood was down. All was going well until I suddenly noticed that it had burst into flames. I was convinced that the petrol tank was about to blow up, but Siggi made me pull the hood up so that we could get at the burning cloth. It cost me £500 to replace it. A few weeks later I drove it to Taunton, not realizing that the wiring had burnt out until smoke appeared from the dashboard. By then I'd really had enough, so I part exchanged it for a beautiful Silver Shadow, losing yet more money over the deal.

I must admit that what went wrong with this one really wasn't the car's fault. Mike and I were appearing on Larry Grayson's Christmas show at Elstree Studios, and Eamonn Andrews was due to make his surprise entrance with the big red book for Larry's *This Is Your Life*. It was a great night and Larry, Danny La Rue and I were the last to leave. I was in no fit state to drive, so Siggi took the wheel. I wasn't even sober enough to realize that she shouldn't have been driving, either. Apparently we got lost on the way home and I remember hearing a few clunking and scraping noises as we reversed our way out of a dead end. The next thing I remember was being rudely awakened from my drunken slumber by the sound of police sirens. I was being sick in the street when a posse of policemen arrived, having been called by the irate owners of several smashed cars in the dead-end street. I was told afterwards that I'd threatened never to do a police concert again, but it seems they were relieved rather than worried.

When I finally emerged from my 'coma' the following day I went down to the police station to see the car. The front of it looked fine, but the rest of it looked as though it had been jammed through a shredder. I didn't even want to start to think about how much it would cost to fix. Then came all the claims from the poor people who lived in the street. I tried to get the Rolls repaired on the cheap but it was a disastrous job, so I decided the only thing to do was to sell it off. Siggi was very lucky – she was only disqualified from driving for a year – we deserved a lot worse and we've never made the same mistake again.

Undeterred, I bought another Silver Shadow – this time a brand-new one. I was really looking forward to taking it to the South of France and driving along the Riviera. The ferry trip was fine, but a hundred miles into France the lights went out. I tried to fix them, but only managed to fuse the whole electrical system. When I went to speak to Siggi through the passenger window I noticed there was a massive great dent in the door. It must have happened on the ferry, but I hadn't seen it until that point. I felt like crying. I did drive the car along the Riviera, but only in one direction so that people couldn't see the dent on the other side.

Fortunately in time Schnorbitz got her own car: a Granada Estate sponsored by Godfrey Davis. So there's no point in my having a Roller any more, and strangely enough the Granada's been thoroughly reliable and never got a mark on it.

I've also had some beautiful houses. Following the one in Whetstone, north London that I bought with the loan from my film star days I moved to an enormous house in Cockfosters, Hertfordshire. I named it Jazzboat II in honour of one of my movies, and we had a lovely life there. It had lots of rooms and beautiful grounds, and we threw massive parties for our friends. What with gardeners, cleaners and heating bills it cost £200 per week to run, which is a lot of money nowadays let alone fifteen years ago.

There was one tragedy that happened there that still haunts me. It involved my Boxer dog Butch. He loved living there: he had a huge garden to chase rabbits and squirrels in, and spent most of his days digging yet another hole under the fence so that he could wander round the neighbourhood. He would take our Alsation Ella with him and they did the rounds of local friends together, stopping off here for tea and there for biscuits and enjoying themselves enormously. They would always be back for dinner by six o'clock on the dot, so when one night they didn't appear I got worried. I covered their normal route but the trail dried up, and by the time I got back home Ella had returned. She was filthy dirty, shaking and in obvious distress. I'd heard stories of young children tying dogs to trees in nearby Hadley Woods and went there to search for Butch, but to no avail. The next morning I went back there and found someone who'd spotted the two of them going in the direction of the station. Staff at the station confirmed they had seen a Boxer and an Alsatian but couldn't tell me where they had gone. I was frantic and spent the next two days searching everywhere I could think of. It was so unlike Butch not to find his way home that I knew something must be wrong.

The following morning I got a phone call from the local police asking me if I owned a dog called Butch. I was so relieved because I thought they had found him, but when they came to the house all they brought was his collar and identity disc. Butch had been tied with a short rope to the railway track, and by the time the inevitable happened his collar was all that was left. The culprits were never found, and sometimes I frighten myself thinking of what I might have done if they had been.

But back to the good times. Of course my best friend other than Siggi is my son Ray. I don't claim to have been the world's greatest father. In fact, for many years while he was growing up I hardly saw him at all as I was mostly away working. But we made up for it in the summer months when Siggi and Ray would come to stay with me wherever we might be appearing in Britain. We did a lot of normal things together, though, like playing with toy cars and soldiers, and quite early on – really to indulge my love of football – I bought him a World Cup edition of the table soccer game, Subbuteo. In 1976 we set up our league division – I would commentate on the games as we played them. Oddly enough, season after season our local Barnet Football Club always seemed to finish as our League Champions. Schnorbitz and I have often been known to stop off at Ray's house in more recent yeras to get in a quick game.

A lot of my friends envy my relationship with Ray and they often offer to buy him from me. He's a wonderfully sensible man and during the last ten years we have grown very close – but I wouldn't sell him; I love him too much. I don't know where he got his good sense from, quite honestly. He's never been the least bit interested in show business, even though when he was a youngster I encouraged him to sing and dance and tell jokes. I think he felt that show business was all right in its place, but he determined to make a 'proper living' when he was still very young. He left school at eighteen and went straight to work in the City. Before long he was completely financially independent, and now he's a successful investment banker dealing with millions of pounds every day. I don't understand exactly what he does – but I know he's very good at it, and I'm very proud of him.

It's a peculiar thing, but I think that as time has gone on we've almost changed roles, with him becoming more the father figure. There have been two incidents which really brought that fact home to me. The first was when Ray was fourteen and had come home from school one day crying, because the sports master had threatened to beat him. I remember being so angry at the time that I went straight to the school the following morning, hunted down the offending master and knocked him flat on his back.

In 1990, Ray did a similar thing for me. As usual, we were invited to the Water Rats' annual ball. I was most unhappy to discover that I'd been relegated to a table right at the back of the hall – in this case an enormous banqueting room at the Grosvenor House Hotel in London's Park Lane, so that trying to see the cabaret from where we were sitting was almost impossible. I'd have had a better view if I'd been sitting on the roof of Guildford Town Hall, thirty miles away. Every time Siggi moved her seat to try to see the stage a particularly uncivil waiter would push her aside. Naturally, I got very angry and told him 'If you do that once more to my wife I'll let you have it.' Within seconds Ray had jumped to his feet, lifted the waiter six inches off the floor and carried him out of the room to dispose of him. It was the only time in my entire life that I've known Ray get at all violent, and it seemed finally to seal our change of role in relation to each other.

I'm delighted to say that in 1990 Ray married a lovely girl called Tina. He continued the tradition that Mike and I started of marrying a non-Jewish woman, but happily he had none of the opposition that we'd had. Tina nearly didn't make the wedding. She works in the City too, and had to deliver a lecture in Helsinki the day before they got married. Just as Ray was putting the final touches to his bachelorhood he got a frantic phone call from Tina saying that she'd missed her return flight and the next available flight would not get her back in time.

We had horrible visions of having to cancel all the arrangements: the Registry Office, the Inn on the Park, the catering, the band and the guests. How do you possibly stop hundreds of guests from turning up at only a moment's notice? Not to be deterred, the Ray and Bernie partnership sprang into action. We told Tina to catch the next flight and sorted out how to cut corners at our end. Ray arranged for the wedding car to pick up Tina's bridal outfit from her home and take it to Heathrow Airport, while I hoped and prayed that British Airways officials would recognize my name and pull a few strings for me. Luckily they did, and the limousine was allowed on to the tarmac to collect Tina from the plane and race her to the Registry Office in Marylebone Road.

We all stood nervously outside on the steps with our fingers crossed, waiting for her to arrive, and couldn't believe it when the limo pulled up and she stepped out looking as though she'd just left a beauty parlour rather than the somewhat cramped changing conditions in the back of the car. Now I'm very happy to say that they're planning to start a family.

Now that I'm not so well it's nice to be able to say that our relationship has deepened into one of real friendship, where we can open our hearts to one another and share our closest secrets. He spends as much time with me as he possibly can and calls several times a day to find out how I am. He's even adopted for me the pet name that I used for my father – 'Mougie', the Russian word for naughty boy.

12

CANCER, THE
FIRST TIME

I'D had a BUPA check-up at the end of 1989, which I passed
with flying colours. I'd been told to lose a bit of weight, which
I'd done, so all was hunky-dory. 'You're marvellous for your
age,' was how they described me. So when I started to get
stomach pains a few months later it never occurred to me that
it could be anything remotely serious, and the doctors didn't
think so either. In May Siggi and I were due to go on a yachting
holiday, sailing around Majorca with two very good friends. I've
grown to love those trips; long, relaxing days sunbathing and
eating wonderful food in utterly luxurious surroundings, and
then great nights at a local restaurant wherever we moored on
the island.

This time it wasn't so good, though. I'd complained to my GP
about what felt like a mixture of cramp and wind and he thought
I must have some kind of gastric bug and prescribed me
antibiotics. But they didn't do much good. I found myself having
to sleep a lot during the day and nothing I did got rid of the
pains, so I ended up trying to get through the holiday rather
than enjoying it. I knew something was wrong, but never
dreamt that it could be serious as my MOT had gone so well.
My GP didn't think so either, and he wasn't the only doctor to
be flummoxed by the persistence of the pains. He gave me

another batch of antibiotics when I got back, but after a while it was apparent that they weren't doing any good at all.

Eventually I went to see Siggi's doctor, Mark Ormston, who is also a friend of the family. He tested my blood and said he thought I might be a little anaemic, so he gave me some B_{12} injections. They seemed to help for a while, but then the pains got faster and more furious and he sent me for a barium meal. In fact I had two – front and back – and they seemed to suggest that something was wrong with my colon: some sort of colitis. I'd never heard of it, but when I mentioned it at my golf club it seemed as though everyone there had either had it themselves or knew someone with it. At first I was relieved finally to put a name to the problem, especially as it seemed that if I ate the right kind of foods, like porridge and bran, and avoided anything with pips in I could do a lot to help myself. But it wasn't long before I realized that none of it was doing any good. At the same time I was trying to work through all this – rehearsing for the Queen Mother's ninetieth birthday celebrations and chasing round the country for various personal appearances. When I was actually performing I could forget the pain, but most of the time it seemed to be eating away at me.

It's funny what you'll do when you're in pain. It got so bad at one stage that I visited a faith healer. It's not that I don't believe in them – in fact I'd never really bothered to think about them one way or another – but by now I was ready to try anything and so I went to see a little old lady in St John's Wood. She was absolutely charming. She recognized me, which always makes me feel better anyway, and felt various bits of my body to try and locate the source of the pain. Eventually she too decided that I had a colitis problem, and gave me a coloured liquid to drink. So what with coloured liquids and a change of diet I thought I had to get better.

But no. By July it was obvious that whatever was wrong with me it wasn't colitis, so it was back to the doctor's, this time at the London Clinic just off Harley Street. I had several X-rays as well as an examination in a big X-ray tube, and I was just beginning to think that it was going to be too expensive to be ill when they told me, 'You're perfect, absolutely fine. If anything, your gall bladder is slightly small.' I don't think I'd ever been so relieved in my life – a small gall bladder I could cope with. But the specialist, Dr Naughton-Morgan, was still mystified as to why I should be in so much pain and decided that the best course of action was to open me up to get a better look, as well as to sort out the gall bladder.

Somehow things were starting to look rosier – it would just be a small operation and I'd only be in hospital for a few days. Little did I know. In fact it seemed so unimportant at the time that Siggi and I debated whether we should leave it until after my birthday on 6 September, when I'd planned to have a big party, or get it over and done with beforehand. She won and we settled on 14 August (Naughton-Morgan had suggested the 13th, but Siggi refused point-blank). So, thus fixed up, I went back to work.

I suppose it's ironic in a way that, completely unaware that I had cancer myself, I was taking part in the Queen Mother's ninetieth birthday gala in aid of the Bud Flanagan Leukaemia Fund. It was a magnificent day, however. I've always loved doing things for the royals, and even the pain couldn't ruin this occasion. The world and its brother were there for the march past and I was surrounded by little children dressed as miniature Bud Flanagans. The band played 'Underneath the Arches' as we made our way up Whitehall and past the Queen Mother. I was so moved that I found myself waving to her and wishing her a happy birthday. I don't know why – it was still too early for her birthday, but I felt that I had to say something. By the time the orchestra started playing 'Strolling' and the choir sang and the crowds cheered, I was in tears. It was such an honour to be invited to be a part of the celebrations for someone as wonderful as the Queen Mother. She once told me that when she saw me play Bud Flanagan it brought back happy memories of her husband and the times they'd spent together enjoying Flanagan and Allen. That alone made it all worthwhile.

A few weeks later Leslie Crowther and I performed as Flanagan and Allen again for the Royal Gala at the Palladium. It really was the night of a thousand stars. Sir John Mills was there with Sir Richard Attenborough, Placido Domingo, Roger Moore, Michael Caine, and numerous others. I sat in the theatre all day just watching all the stars coming on to the stage to rehearse their bits and bobs. I will always remember that day, even though I was in pain – it was an incredible experience, especially seeing Michael Caine and Roger Moore.

The strange thing about rehearsals is that you don't have an audience – it sounds an obvious thing to say, but for someone who isn't used to doing a stage act it can be quite a daunting experience. You have to stand on stage and deliver supposedly funny lines and all you hear is silence. All the other people in the theatre are too involved with what they're doing, so there's no one to laugh at you. So when Michael Caine came off stage after his rehearsal he was frantic. 'It's not funny. We weren't funny at all. We can't do the act. It's a disaster.' He came and found me at the back of the stalls. 'You know about comedy,' he said. 'You've been doing it all your life. What do we do if they don't laugh – we'll die.' Well, he was completely wrong – their piece *was* funny. I told him that just having him and Roger up on stage together was like gold and that they really couldn't fail. 'No, no,' he said. 'I don't fancy this at all, all this live stuff. I shouldn't be doing this. I can't remember the words. Bloody hell, what are we going to do?' Anyway, Roger and I took him to the green room, where eventually he calmed down.

When the curtain went up that night Leslie and I got a brilliant response; the audience cheered and yelled. It was fabulous, and for the first time that day I wasn't in pain. As soon as he came off, though, I ran over the road to the pub to get myself two large vodkas to try to keep it away. I got back to the theatre just in time to see Michael and Roger do their piece from the side of the stage. They were wonderful. As Michael came off he thanked me for helping him relax and toasted me with champagne in his dressing room. 'That Bernie Winters,' he said, 'he was the only one that knew. He was the one that said we'd do well.' As if that wasn't enough, to cap it all, the great theatre impresarios Lord Bernard Delfont and Louis Benjamin complimented me on how good the Flanagan and Allen spot had been. Louis said to me, 'You get more like Bud Flanagan every day. I can't tell the difference any more.'

I'll always be grateful that I managed to do those gala performances before getting too ill. I know I've said it before, but it was truly an honour to be invited to take part and it's a very precious memory to me. So much so that I went into hospital a happy and optimistic man. When I woke up in the recovery room after the operation I was still blissfully unaware that I had cancer and that, instead of losing a gall bladder, I was now minus two-thirds of my stomach and half my colon. What I *was* aware of, though, were the tubes and pipes coming out of every part of my body. Any place there was a hole spare for a tube, one was there – up my nose, in my ears, my mouth, all the way up my sides. I looked like a stuffed pig and my tongue felt like the Gobi Desert. I was so desperate for a cup of tea that I tried to bribe one of the nurses, a fabulous girl called Carmel Gordon, with promises of glamorous champagne nights out at Stringfellow's nightclub. She didn't fall for it, unfortunately.

I found out later that Siggi and Ray knew about the cancer straightaway but didn't tell me for another five days. They must have been feeling desperate but were by my side all the time being cheerful and supportive, and they didn't give a thing away. Siggi told the doctors in no uncertain terms that as soon as it was practical I should be told the truth. She can be very forceful when necessary. In fact, since the illness started I've renamed her Arnold Schwarzenegger. She's had a lot to be strong about, too. Our friends were obviously concerned to know how I was, but she couldn't tell them the truth before I was told and so it was difficult for her to talk to them. Also she was worried about news getting out to the papers; cancer is such a taboo subject that even if I recovered I might never be offered work again. So she had all that to cope with while acting towards me as though everything was normal. I thank God that she had Ray, who's been a tower of strength since the illness started. He's been a good friend to me too.

A few years earlier, while Siggi and I were away on holiday, Ray thought he'd do me a favour by taking my Rolls in for servicing. Nice idea, but he obviously hadn't realized how much a full service on a Rolls-Royce costs – it's a luxury most Roller owners can't afford. I came back to find the car gleaming in the driveway, and when I drove it it purred along like a dream. Then Ray told me how much I owed the garage. His face fell when I reacted. 'Two grand?' I yelled. 'Not two grand!' I said the very same thing as I regained consciousness after my stomach operation. Ray was leaning over me and asking how I felt. 'Not too grand,' I said.

During the five days after the operation I seemed to be constantly dipping in and out of consciousness; the tubes were taking over all my bodily functions and I couldn't eat or drink or move. I know that everyone says it, but the nurses were fantastic. They had to shave me and wash me, even clean my teeth: I was completely incapacitated. Siggi and Ray had had me moved to a larger room so that all the tubes could fit in, and had hired a male nurse to look after me during the night. I slept very fitfully, and the strange shadows that the night light threw on the walls gave me bad dreams. I couldn't wait for daylight. At one point I think I might have been delirious – I saw the nurse moving about the room with a torch and it frightened me. I told him to get out, thinking he was a burglar.

Eventually Siggi broke the news and I remember her words like it was yesterday. 'You've been very ill,' she said. 'It wasn't your gall bladder, it was cancer, and you're very lucky to be here. You nearly died during the operation, so now you've got to take it very steady.' Apparently, rather than the expected hour and a half the operation had taken eight hours. In fact it had gone on for so long that the anaesthetist's car had been clamped.

To say that I was devastated by the news would be an understatement. Obviously I knew that the operation had been more serious than we'd thought, but I'd had no idea I had cancer. It was an absolute bombshell and I felt numb and petrified at the same time. Strangely enough, after the initial shock I didn't think I was going to die. Like most other people I'd always thought that cancer meant certain death, but to my surprise I found I was quite hopeful, especially since at last I was no longer in pain. Siggi explained that the diseased part of my stomach had been removed and so I felt as though the worst was already over: the cancer had been cut out, so I was bound to be all right.

During this time I was allowed no visitors other than Siggi, Ray and Tina. The doctor had thought it best for me to have complete rest for a few weeks while I recovered from the operation. Fortunately that didn't stop people writing and phoning, and getting their messages and cards really cheered me up. Lionel Blair phoned every day, Cilla Black told me she loved me so much I had to get better, and Bob Monkhouse would send me cards with his own jokes in. Bob's warmth and generosity have been a constant source of strength to me throughout my illness, and he's proved to be an invaluable friend. Tarby called up to make me laugh and my friend Ray Stevens even posed as a doctor to get into the hospital. It's at times like this you really appreciate your friends.

Ray Stevens was kindness itself throughout my illness, both in hospital and later. As well as calling me twice a day to see how I was he lent Siggi and me his villa for recuperation. We didn't fly down in his Lear jet – we went on a scheduled flight

– but he helped with transport at the other end. Before we took off we met an old acquaintance whom I'm not particularly keen on. He very flashily told us that he was flying club class and would see us when we landed. So I particularly enjoyed sitting on the front seat in the club section and having a special bus meet us from the plane in Spain.

After a week I was allowed my first taste of water. Nothing had passed my lips up to that point, and the thirst I had was indescribable. Friends had sent me bottles of champagne and baskets of fruit to wish me well, and all I could do was stare at them – it was absolute agony. The taste of the first tiny droplet of water the nurse put on my lips was like nectar. The next day Dr Naughton-Morgan came to see me. He told me that it would be another six weeks before I was able to eat, and described what to expect when I finally did. He explained that as most of my stomach had gone, food would literally drop down inside me rather than go slowly through the intestine. The not quite medical term for it is 'dump-back'. Then because it may not be properly digested, it would probably try to come back up again. 'Heaving', it's called. So I had a lot to look forward to; dumping and heaving, only eating tiny twiddly bits of food at a time or it would hurt like hell, and sticking to things that are easily digested like custards, soups, etc. The strangest thing was that my father had had exactly the same kind of experience. I didn't know why at the time, but I remember that it was a constant source of amusement to the rest of us whenever he ate and heaved or dumped. Apparently after six months or so your stomach starts to stretch again, which makes it easier to eat. So while I wasn't entirely delighted about my prospects for the near future, I still managed to be optimistic. That is until Naughton-Morgan broke his second piece of news: 'And in the next couple of days Dr Price, the Clinic's cancer specialist, will be coming to see you.'

I've got to know Len Price quite well now and like him very much. He made his way into my room that day, past all the pipes and tubes, and sat down next to the bed. 'How you feeling, boyo?'

I nodded: 'Okay.'

'Do you drink?' he asked me.

'Well, I would if I didn't have all these things hanging out of my mouth,' I said.

'Shame you can't have a Scotch,' he said. 'Do you smoke?'

I gave him the same answer again, and he said, 'Shame you can't have a fag, because this cancer has a 90 per cent chance of coming back and a 10 per cent chance of not coming back.'

I said, 'Well, that's not very good – 10 per cent is the commission you give to an agent. It's not very much.'

He explained to me that there was a tiny bit of cancer left, and if I were to go for chemotherapy immediately after I'd recovered from the operation, in about four days, I'd be giving myself a 50 per cent chance of getting rid ot it. The import of what he was saying began to sink in and I started to cry, but I agreed to the treatment. After all, if my 50 per cent chance of getting rid of it came up then I'd have a 100 per cent chance of surviving. With odds like that, you don't have any option.

What I really didn't want to do was to stay in hospital, so I decided to discharge myself. The tubes and pipes and stitches had already been removed, so I rang Ray to ask him to book me a car and Siggi to tell her I was coming home. The sister was horrified when she came into my rom and saw me ready to leave. 'You can't possibly go yet. You haven't recovered.'

'No, no,' I said, 'the doctor said I can go.'

She knew I was lying and called Naughton-Morgan down. I told him that I couldn't face going straight for chemotherapy without first going home to build up my strength. Eventually he agreed, on condition that I took all my pills and potions with me. I had no strength to do anything at home, but just lay in bed or on the sofa in the living room. I didn't mind. It was such a relief to be out of that hospital room, away from the nightmares and with my family and dogs. By the time I had to go back to the Clinic three days later I felt rejuvenated and positive that the treatment was going to work.

My first question on seeing Dr Price again was whether or not I was going to lose my hair. He told me that the type of chemotherapy he was going to give me for the first two treatments was a fairly strong one and that there was indeed a possibility of hair loss. That upset me enormously, and I was in tears when I rang Siggi to tell her. She made me laugh by saying she'd bring in a selection of blond wigs for me to try – sometimes humour is the only way to cope. I had no idea what to make of chemotherapy before it started. I envisaged a sort of Frankenstein's laboratory, but in fact it was all very simple: a controlled drip was fed into my arm through a needle inserted in a vein. Because of the sedatives I slept for the first twelve hours or so and woke up to find that the veins in my arm had turned black – a very odd experience, but at least I was fairly mobile. I could get up to shave or go to the loo so long as I took my friendly drip stand with me. After thirty-six hours water was flushed through me to wash all the chemicals out, and at that stage I started to feel pretty uncomfortable; I wanted to pee every ten minutes, and then started to get sudden and uncontrollable attacks of diarrhoea. Whenever I soiled the bed the nurses would come in with protective gloves, remove my pyjamas and bedclothes and take them away to be burnt – it's the only way to cope with the radioactivity.

What I didn't realize was that the drugs would make my mind wander. I felt as though I was on some kind of happy pill, or in loo-lah land as Siggi put it. She said it was like talking to a piece of cheese – it sounded sensible at the time, but afterwards she realized that I hadn't been in the least bit aware of what I'd been saying. Very wisely, she ignored me over the next five treatments. Ray on the other hand would sit for hours having long conversations with me, and come back the next day and tell me how much he'd enjoyed it. I never remembered a thing. It was being in that state of mind which got me into trouble.

I still hadn't decided exactly who should know about the cancer. Siggi continued to field calls from the press as well as from acquaintances. She'd told the family and our closest friends, but realized from the reactions of some of them that the word 'cancer' is still socially unacceptable – some of them told her that they didn't want to know, that they couldn't handle it, and shied away. That made it difficult for her to know who to tell, and especially whether or not it should become general knowledge. Then I made a bit of a blunder and the whole story was out.

I was listening to the Michael Parkinson radio programme on LBC one morning and heard him say that his guest interviewee had pulled out, so I rang up to offer my services. Much to the nurse's disquiet I spoke to his production office to say that I was in the London Clinic and really not doing an awful lot, so if Michael wanted to call me back I'd be happy to have a chat with him. The phone rang and within minutes I was on air in my loo-lah land state, telling Michael how wonderful all the nurses were and how much better I was feeling. I told him I knew I shouldn't have this nurse in bed with me and was generally larking about, but carefully avoiding the word 'cancer'. Then, without thinking, I told him and the rest of London that I was having chemotherapy. I'd blown it.

It took about three minutes for the newspapers to get on the phone. The next day the world and its brother knew I had stomach cancer. Oddly enough, despite all the indecision beforehand when the news finally broke I didn't mind. In fact it was a relief – I'm not very good at bottling things up. At last I could answer all the questions and say, 'Yes, I've got cancer and I'm going to fight it – and not only that, I'm going to beat it.' Then, when all the letters and cards started to arrive from well-wishers, it gave me an incredible lift. Just seeing the piles and piles of get-well messages from people I've never even met was wonderful. They'll never know how much their kindness helped give me the strength to get through those treatments.

I had six in all, with a two-week gap between each. As soon as I came out of hospital after one I would be waiting around the the for the next, and often I'd still be in loo-lah land. It was easy to forget how weak I was from the operation, let alone from the chemotherapy. One Saturday morning, about twelve hours after finishing a heavy chemotherapy session, I got a call from Thames Television asking me if I'd go along and take part in a couple of *Give Us a Clue*s. Bombed out of my brain I agreed, and they sent a car to collect me. I was dressed and ready to leave with my suitcase when Siggi came back home. 'What on earth are you doing?' she said, seeing me standing there as though I was about to move out. When I told her she stared at me in utter disbelief. 'But you can't possibly go and do two shows,' she said. 'You're spaced out – you don't know what you're doing.'

So war broke out in the Winters household. I insisted I was going to do it, and told Siggi that she didn't have to come with me because I was going anyway. In the end she did come. In fact she cancelled the Thames Television car and drove me in herself. Anyway, everything went well; they gave me a wonderful dressing room, everyone was very helpful and made a real fuss of me, and my performance made me look really quite normal. I saw one of them go out on television and I seemed to make quite good sense.

After each chemotherapy treatment I'd spend a couple of days being not only slightly doo-lally but also feeling giddy, sick and having diarrhoea; after that period I'd be desperate to get back to normal. I was starting to look a lot better; my hair hadn't fallen out – I checked it every day to make sure, and my appetite was getting back to normal so I was starting to put weight back on which made me look a lot healthier. While staying at Ray Stevens' Spanish villa I took full advantage of the food and got a lot fitter, swimming in the pool every day and resting in the sunshine. I wanted to play golf as well, but trying to swing a club brought home to me how fragile my wounds still were from the operation, and so I had to limit myself to gentle games on the putting green.

I was also gearing up for *Aladdin* in Basildon that Christmas. Siggi and Ray were convinced I shouldn't do it and the producer called me, sure that I'd have to pull out, but I was determined. I had my clothes altered to fit the new, slimmer-lined me and knew I could overcome the loss of power in my voice. Everything seemed to be going so well. The regular blood tests that were taken to see whether the chemotherapy treatment was working gave good signs each time, and for the first time in months I felt wonderfully pain-free.

Siggi and I got into a sort of routine where we'd have lunch at Langan's just before I went into the Clinic for the treatment. One day Michael Caine was there at his usual table. I hadn't seen him since the gala and he was obviously thrown by how much thinner I looked. 'Hello, Bernie. Cor, you've lost a ton of weight. What you got – AIDS?'

For want of anything better to say I told him, 'No, cancer.'

'Oh, **** me, you haven't. I *am* sorry,' he said.

'Actually,' I said, 'I'm trying to lose a lot of weight so that I can become a sex symbol like you and get into the movies.' He was charming as usual and wished me well.

One of my first social outings after the treatment started was to an enormous party thrown by Thames TV to celebrate the 501st edition of *This Is Your Life*. All the people who'd been subjects on the programme over the years were invited, and I sat on a table with my old friends Philip Jones, Jimmy Jewell, Pete Murray and Frankie Vaughan. Siggi was playing my conscientious nurse that night and only allowed me one drink. Maybe she should have been sitting with Oliver Reed, because that was the night that he got into a huge fight with Patrick Mower, and Jackie Pallo and Nosher Powell had to drag him off. Oliver was thrown out and Nosher said to me, 'He's a lovely boy, but he just goes mad sometimes.'

Su Pollard was there too, and when she saw me she ran over

and said, 'Cor, Bernie, you've lost a lot of weight. Been on a diet?' Somebody whispered to her that I had cancer. 'CANCER!' she screamed 'Bloody Hell, not cancer!' If I thought I was going to keep my illness secret, my cover was definitely blown that night. She's a great girl Su, a real character, and I love her very much.

During this time my brother Mike rang me. He'd heard about the illness and so we arranged to meet at the Hilton Hotel at Lord's. He was just over for a few days and we only had an hour together before I went in for treatment, but that was the first time since we'd broken up that we treated each other as real friends again. Since then we've been all right, and I have an open invitation to visit his house in Miami.

The last chemotherapy treatment was in October 1990, and Siggi and I decided that a good holiday in Nassau was in order afterwards with lashings of sunshine, good food and rest before the pantomime. I had to have one of my regular blood tests taken out there, so that we could keep a check on how well we'd beaten the cancer. That one blood test was worse than all the others put together. The fellow couldn't find a vein to put the needle into, and stabbed me all over my arm while he was trying. I nearly killed him, but at least by the time I got back Dr Price could clear me. 'To all intents and purposes you've beaten it and can start living a normal life again,' he said.

I was ecstatic. All the pain and worry had been worth it – I'd had a 50 per cent chance of beating it, and I'd done it. My friend Lou Manzie gave me a diamond horseshoe, and I went on *Wogan* with Schnorbitz to tell everyone that it was possible to beat this horrible disease. At the end of 1990 I could well have been the happiest man in the world. I certainly felt like the luckiest.

13

ONE DAY AT A TIME

SIGGI and Ray tried very hard to talk me out of doing the pantomime, but I felt so wonderful I thought I could do anything and I insisted. At first all went well – I was as good as I ever was on stage and everything was fantastic. After my appearance on *Wogan* I got hundreds more phone calls and letters from people, telling me how pleased they were for me. I even got one from a woman whose son was in the army and had been sent out to fight in the Gulf War; she wrote that seeing me on television had made her feel so much more confident about the safety of her boy.

Even my social life started to pick up again. My friend Ray Stevens was having a party at his house, and Bob Monkhouse and I persuaded him to turn it into a fund-raising occasion for the Stars' Organization for Spastics, of which Bob is chairman. He agreed, and we showed a videotape of the charity's work and the children it helped while Barbara Windsor collected money. We got £5000 and Ray, out of the kindness of his heart, added another £10,000 – an incredibly generous man. In return Bob invited Ray and his wife, Penny, Siggi and me to be guests of honour at the SOS ball at the Hilton Hotel. Ray came to collect us in his Rolls-Royce so that we could all travel into town together and I gave them a drink. After a while I realized that Penny still hadn't taken her coat off, and I thought I could see that all she had on underneath was stockings. She explained that she was only going to put her dress on when we arrived at the Hilton because she didn't want to crease it. What I didn't realize was that she meant she was going to get changed out in the street for all the world to see. Sure enough, Ray parked near the Hilton while Penny leaped out and went round to the boot to get changed. I couldn't believe it – it was the middle of winter, freezing cold and there she was, practically nude, putting her dress on in the middle of the road. Siggi took pictures and I can vouch for Penny's plan – the dress wasn't creased at all. The evening got better and better. Rory Bremner and Victoria Wood were the cabaret, and then my old friend Michael Grade and I called the bingo. It was a great night and illness couldn't have been further from my mind.

Aladdin was going very well. We even had our run extended for another week, but a while before the end I started to get pains again – not the same as before the stomach operation, but sometimes just as severe. Siggi and I both thought I must have pulled a muscle playing golf or performing my Busy Bee sketch in the pantomime. I started taking painkillers before the matinee and then again before the evening performance so that I could get through the shows. Before long I was on eight a day. Then my appetite started to go. I didn't think much of that at first and decided not to worry Siggi with it. But she caught me out one day when she arrived at the theatre and found Schnorbitz with my sandwiches hanging out of her mouth.

Somehow I managed to get through the pantomime and then decided to go back to the London Clinic. I wasn't due for another check-up until the end of February – it was now only mid-January – but we thought I might as well see what was going on. When Dr Naughton-Morgan heard that I'd been in panto he wasn't the least bit suprised to find us there. 'What do you expect?' he said. 'Most people take a year off after an operation like yours, and that's without all the other treatments you've been having.' He prescribed a good rest, so we decided to go skiing. I'd never got back to the weight I'd been before the operation and now I was starting to lose a little bit more, so David Vine, the sports commentator, introduced me to one of his skiing outfitter contacts to get togged out with new gear and brand-new boots.

I was really looking forward to the holiday. We'd booked ourselves into the Crystal, a fabulous hotel in Obergurgl with panoramic views over the mountains – the snow was good too. I tried to ski two or three times but didn't really have the strength. When I fell over it hurt, so I spent most of the time sitting on the hotel balcony halfway up the mountain trying to catch the sun. I assumed that I couldn't ski because I was tired and that I'd wrenched some muscles or strained the stitches that were still inside me from the operation, but then I wondered why I could hardly eat anything.

For the first three days I lived on strudel and custard, the only things I could get down and keep there. The head waiter at the hotel was devastated – I'd order a five-course meal, but as soon as he brought the first course I'd be off to the toilet to throw up. Soon even the thought of food made me want to be sick – only by that time I was just retching, with nothing in my stomach. He tried really hard, saying that he'd get me anything I wanted; we tried various things, but it was no good. Siggi would take me to different restaurants, sometimes more than one a night, to try to find something that would appeal to me. Normally I love German and Austrian food, but the more I thought about eating the worse I got. By day four even the strudel and custard became impossible and I couldn't find anything I could drink either. Ray, made his usual check call that day to see how I was, and when I told him he said he'd get me on a flight home immediately. 'What are you talking about?' I said, 'I can't leave yet. I mean I'm Jewish and I've paid for another eight days.' He said he'd ring back the next day, and if I was no better I was coming home.

I really couldn't work out what was wrong with me. I knew it couldn't be the cancer – my stomach had been cut out and the rest of it had been cleared with chemotherapy, so that was impossible. But I was in a lot of pain and couldn't eat, so something was obviously wrong. I was relieved the next day when Ray phoned and told me that we were booked on the 2 p.m. flight from Munich. It had taken Siggi three days to pack our bags before the holiday. It took her three minutes to pack them to come home. Within an hour she'd returned our skis to the hire shop, settled the hotel bill, booked a cab and got us ready to leave. The hotel staff were very upset, convinced we were leaving because of something they'd done, but she explained that I wasn't well and that we had to go home. The cab driver was magnificent: it was a three-and-a-half-hour drive across the German–Austrian border to the airport, and he got us there in good time to check in. The security was massive because of the Gulf War, and even though Siggi's German herself she ended up swearing at the officials who were checking each item of our baggage with meticulous thoroughness. She knew they were right, but she was desperate to get me somewhere comfortable because I was in so much pain. Ray had booked us club seats, and when we got on the plane we discovered that the stewardess looking after us was a friend of Lou Manzie's. She plied us with champagne and brandies which I suddenly found I could drink, and Siggi watched me in a trance as I gobbled the food and then looked at her tray in case she had left anything. My first meal was prawn salad and a roll – I remember it to this day. It was the first thing I'd eaten for a week.

The following day I went back to the Clinic. Dr Naughton-Morgan sent me for an X-ray which showed nothing, and then for a scan. That's an amazing experience. You lie on a table and next to you is a monitor, like a television screen. They rub your stomach with grease and then examine it with this thing that looks like a razor head and which has got a camera inside it. Up on the screen come pictures of your insides and it's just incredible – it looks like an undersea world; I kept expecting

Jacques Cousteau to swim by. After the scan Naughton-Morgan sent for me and told me pretty bluntly that I had cancer again. I couldn't believe it; I'd just got rid of it. I mean it was only a matter of two months since I'd been cleared – it was a bit quick to get it again. 'It's in one or two areas as well,' he went on.

'Blimey!' I said, 'one or two areas.' I mean if it had been two or three, I wouldn't be here now.

He sent me two doors down Harley Street to see Dr Price. His advice was that I should come back into the Clinic the next day because I had cancer of the liver. I felt like saying, 'Cancer of the liver, bacon, sausage and egg, by the sound of it.' He told me that the chemotherapy he'd be putting me on this time would be much tougher, and that generally people couldn't take more than two treatments. It was exactly like the first time; cancer couldn't have been further from my mind, and when I was told it all happened so fast I didn't have time to think. At first, that is.

Dr Price was right about the treatment – it was a thousand times worse than the previous ones. You're all right while it's happening, but the after-effects are practically unbearable. The difference this time was that after the chemicals are washed through platinum is then fed into your veins for two hours. It's not normally painful unless you have constipation, and unfortunately I did have constipation. At the stage where you're washed through, everything is released: that was awful. I felt incontinent and ashamed, but as ever the nurses were magnificent.

That was nothing, though, compared to how I felt when I came home. Food, any type of food, smelled like garbage. I just couldn't eat a thing other than the occasional single slice of thin toast. My body was disintegrating in front of my eyes until the skin was hanging off me; my muscles were like tissue paper and I had no strength at all. My voice was so weak I could hardly speak and I was literally crawling around the house. Siggi was frantic. She kept buying and preparing different kinds of food in the hope that she'd find something I could eat, but nothing worked.

In February 1990, twelve months before, I had weighed fourteen stone. After the treatment I lost eight pounds in what seemed like two minutes and went down to under ten stone. I looked like a bag of bones. Dr Price had warned me that I could lose up to half a stone per treatment, and by this stage I knew I was too weak to contemplate a second one. In fact I thought it was quite likely that I'd have disappeared by then. For the first time I started to think that I might not be able to beat the cancer again. I'd been so proud of getting rid of it in my stomach, but now I had serious doubts about making it through this one in my liver. It was like having survived the first round against Mike Tyson, thinking it was all over but then being sent back in for another ten. At that stage I gave myself five to one that I wouldn't be alive for the second treatment.

After ten days like this and twenty-one days of not eating I went back to see Dr Price. I think he was surprised to see how much I'd deteriorated physically. He asked me if I could get out of a chair without using my arms to push me up, and I couldn't. I asked him if I was going to die and he said, 'I hope not. We'll do everything we can to make sure you don't.' He also told me that I'd have to be stronger before the next treatment and that steroids would help me with that. I knew I had to have the treatment because there's no alternative with liver cancer. It's not like the stomach – it can't be taken out.

(*What follows is Bernie's taped diary entries during the last stage of his illness, which he made as and when he was strong enough.*)

1 March

I've been on the steroids for nearly two weeks now and I feel much stronger. Dr Price won't give me any odds on this cancer

– no fifty-fifties this time; and he won't be able to tell if the chemotherapy's working until after the second treatment. At least I feel more able to take another one now, but I must admit I'm a lot more uncertain this time. With the cancer in my stomach I never felt this bad, and I knew I was going to win. Now I'm not so sure. I do know that I don't want to die, though. I passed a funeral procession today and found myself wondering if that would be me soon, but I have to stop thinking like that. There's no room for negative thoughts. I need all my strength to fight.

I watched Marti Caine on television the other day talking about her illness. She had cancer as well, and I can relate to her problem but not to her attitude. When they told her she had five years to live she was grateful. I'd hate to know how long I had left. It really would be like a death sentence. I mean, what would you do? My life is already wonderful: my wife, my son, my friends, my work. I wouldn't want to change any of it. All I want is to carry on living it, to be stronger so that I can. If it really was the end I wouldn't want to be told – I'd just want someone to slip a few more drugs into the chemotherapy drip and off I'd trot. I'm not a quitter.

I always remember sitting with my great friend Matt Monro when he was dying. Just before he went into his final coma he was talking enthusiastically about going to Florida, having parties, going to clubs, living a normal, full life – and he was even smoking a cigarette. Death couldn't have been further from his mind. The television was on, and when the news announced that Matt Monro was fighting for his life in a London hospital he said, 'What on earth are they talking about?' That's what I'm like. I want the good life to keep going until the end, and I don't want to know that I'm going to die.

I'm pretty well incapacitated now. I only leave the house for the odd short walk with the dogs and to visit the Clinic. Today I should have been playing golf in Blackheath for the Bernie Winters Cancer Research Charity, but I'm too weak. Pete

Murray is very kindly standing in for me, but I wish I was there. I've had to cancel my tour with Vince Hill as well, which is a shame, but hopefully it won't be long before I can start work again and Siggi and I can take all the trips we've had to postpone – like Ray Stevens' invitations to stay at the George V Hotel in Paris, go racing at Longchamps and have lunch in Venice. There's still so much to look forward to, like Arsenal winning the cup – I want to be there for that. George Graham, the Arsenal manager, promised me tickets if they got to the final.

Siggi and I had some friends round last night to celebrate the end of the Gulf War and our thirty-third anniversary. We had to keep it short because I get so tired, but it was a lovely evening and I felt so normal by the end of it. When we came back down to earth, Siggi was very upset at the thought that we may not have many more nights like it. But we both realized that we should count our blessings about how lucky I have been, compared with the boys who died in the Gulf. They were so young and hardly had the chance to live any of their lives. I've had fifty-eight years, so really I shouldn't complain. Somewhere deep in my soul I feel that I'm going to survive this; even though I'm not very strong, I'm sure it won't beat me. At least I hope not. When I do recover – and if it takes six treatments, I'll have six – I'll be back trying to help cancer research again with 'Look at me, I've beaten it.'

At least out of all this badness has come one wonderful thing – I'm brothers with Mike again now. It's so stupid really that it's taken this kind of illness to bring us back together again, but at least it's happened. He was over for a short while to have some treatment for his own illness – not so much the Winters Brothers, more the Cancer Brothers – and we spent some time reminiscing about the old days and our families and daft things that we've done. It really felt as if there were no barriers between us any more and that we are genuinely friends again. Since he went back to Miami he's called me every day to see how I am, and with any luck I'll be well enough to go and visit him in April. I know our parents would be very happy to think we're a united family again, and so am I. I'm looking forward to seeing him soon. From now on I'm going to write this book as and when I'm strong enough. It's difficult to plan anything at the moment.

8 March

I went into the Clinic on Tuesday for the second chemotherapy treatment, and hopefully the last. They put me straight to bed with the drip in my arm and gave me some sleeping pills. I slept until three the next morning. Ray and Tina came to see me on Tuesday night, but I was dead to the world. Every six hours on Wednesday the nurses came in to change the fluids in the drip. Siggi and my mother-in-law visited me during the day, then Ray joined me in the evening and we watched the Manchester United v. St Etienne football match and then later the Mason v. Lennox fight. It was quite an enjoyable night's viewing, particularly as Manchester won, and I was ready to sleep again by the time Ray left at eleven but the nurses kept me awake until 4 a.m., until the platinum had been fed into me. I had been constipated until Thursday morning, and then all hell broke loose. The nurses were having to remove the commode every ten minutes and had to change the bed twice. It's soul-destroying to be that incapacitated.

It's Friday now and I came home yesterday evening. It's nice to be home but I'm very weak again, and what little appetite I had has disappeared. I'll keep this short because my voice is practically non-existent. Hopefully this treatment is doing me good. I won't know any results for another ten days – it's a long time to wait. I'll probably be down to nine stone by then, but if it works it's worth it. Anyone else who has to put up with this has my deepest sympathy.

20 March

There's only one word for this platinum chemotherapy – it's a bastard. I had my second go of it a fortnight ago, and I'm only just beginning to get back on my feet again. I'm down to nine stone and feeling very weak. Yesterday I had a call to tell me that I'm booked in for another treatment next Tuesday. It's not the best booking I've ever had, and quite honestly the idea of suffering another two weeks of that treatment – three days of chemotherapy and then ten days of losing another six to eight pounds, to go down to eight stone something – is something I don't think I can take. I was elated last week when I went for my blood test and someone at the Clinic told me that you don't normally have more than two goes at this type of chemotherapy. Well, of course, with news like that I was off and running thinking I'd be out and about again – the lunatic's back! Getting the phone call to tell me I'm having another one has brought me down again with a very big bump, like being hit with an iron door.

Unfortunately Dr Price has had a heart attack and I can't speak to him, so I don't know exactly why he wants me back there next week. Perhaps it's not for the platinum – I just don't know. I also don't know any of the results of my blood tests. They can't actually ascertain whether the treatments are working until after the second one but no one is telling me how I'm doing. It's now five weeks since it all started again and I have no conception of whether I'm getting better, worse or holding. The uncertainty is murder, and there's no one to tell me what's happening. Another doctor visited me while I was in the Clinic, but only to ask me how I was feeling. When I said 'Dreadful' he just said he was sorry, that it was nice to meet me, and then left. I haven't seen him since. I dropped into Dr Price's rooms to see how he was last week, and there was yet another doctor there. I tried to ask her about this constipation that I've got, thinking that she was replacing Dr Price, but all she said was that she didn't know anything about my case and that I should try the Clinic. I don't know who she was – probably a vet or something.

This not knowing is like living on the edge of a precipice and very, very depressing. Mentally you go to pieces. I'm not that strong, and you start thinking of all the terrible things like death. And whereas before I could handle all those things, these days I just can't. The doctors tell you not to get depressed, but how the hell do you stop yourself? How do you cope with it? I get very irritable; nasty to the people who are good to me – my loved ones. Before, with the operation and stomach cancer it was nothing – well, it was big, but no problem as far as I was concerned. There was never any doubt mentally. I was always so convinced and positive. But this one I just don't know, and I hate it.

Sometimes I think it's only the steroids that are keeping me alive. Someone at the Clinic last week told me that they're very habit-forming and hard to get off. Well, I don't want to end up getting rid of cancer and becoming a drug addict – I've got enough problems already. So last Saturday I decided to cut the steroids down. Everyone's their own doctor at times, and I thought I could only feel better without them. I had it all planned: I'd only take three or four steroids and have a very enjoyable evening watching the England v. France rugby match where England was going for the Grand Slam.

Siggi told me not to stop the tablets, that they're like antibiotics – you have to stay the course or they don't work, and anyway you have to be weaned off them slowly. Of course I knew better and didn't take them. Within twenty-four hours I'd deteriorated 900 per cent. I couldn't walk – I was staggering and doddering; I had terrible wind and I couldn't breathe. My GP was shocked when he saw me, and when I told him what I'd done he immediately made me take five steroids, then another three. I won't try that again in a hurry; and if anyone in a similar situation is reading this just don't stop the steroids because they're amazingly powerful.

I've been having a real problem with constipation as well. Anyone who's ever had it badly will know what it's like – I was writhing around the floor in pain, not knowing where to put myself. The only thing I could do for any relief from it was to get into a steaming hot bath and take every laxative known to man – not that any of them worked. But there's always humour in everything, and while I was having one of these baths, lying there in agony sweating away in a sauna-like room and looking like a drowned herring, Frank Carson rang up – somewhat tired and emotional. He told Siggi that the wreckage of the *Marie Celeste* had been discovered and in it the divers had found the captain's log which told them why the ship had been deserted – he'd just told the passengers that Cannon and Ball were booked for New Year's Eve. Thank you, Frank – it didn't solve my constipation, but it did cheer me up. In fact it was Bob Monkhouse who cured that problem for me. He's had the same problem for years and told me about a preparation you can buy over the counter at a chemist – it's the only one of the dozens of medicines that I've tried that's worked. I'm much relieved, as they say.

After the weekend and the steroid episode I got so low about everything that I agreed to see a faith healer again. I hadn't been terribly impressed by the lady I'd seen in St John's Wood: she was delightful and charming, but hadn't detected my stomach cancer. Even so, I decided to give it another go because nothing else seemed to be working – and anyway, what did I have to lose? Some friends told me about a world-famous man called Leonard Serlin who lives in Stanmore. They said I'd have to ring quickly for an appointment, as he's always so busy.

I had my first appointment with him yesterday and he showed me some very impressive press cuttings about people he's cured all around the world. I told him that I wasn't really a believer, but that I was so down and miserable that I'd try anything to get out of it. I lay down on a settee and he put his hands on me and told me what he was doing as he moved them around. 'I'm now touching your liver. Yes, it's bad. I'm now going into your heart and your gall bladder, your kidneys, some of your bowels.' I have to say that I couldn't feel a thing but he said that I was very relaxed – well, I don't find that hard as an old performer – and after half an hour he told me that I'd responded very well. To be blunt and honest I didn't understand it. To me it's science fiction if someone says, 'I'm going into your heart and operating on it' while they're touching you and you're lying on their settee. It's beyond my comprehension – I'm not intelligent enough to figure it out.

Anyway, we'd arranged that I'd go back this morning, which I did, and he told me then that he'd paid me a trans-visit during the night. Well, of course, I didn't know anything about that – I was fast asleep. Which made me wonder what he'd got up to with my wife, but she said she hadn't felt anything either. This morning I woke up with terrible chest pains, like having a heart attack. I was also feeling very depressed again, but when I arrived at his house he told me I was looking a lot better. He said he was going to operate on my heart, so I lay on his couch and waited. Now, four or five hours later, I must say – to give the man his due – that I feel a whole lot better. He seems to have alleviated a lot of problems though I don't know how he's done it. He said that my liver's responding, and funnily enough I'm not in pain there. In fact I'd assumed my liver was on the left, as that was where I was feeling the pain, but it appears that it's on the right – so maybe the cancer has gone. I don't know. He told me that the pain I was feeling was in my bowels; he felt that area and said I have to believe because he works through God. I said he couldn't possibly have a better agent, and if this works – who knows? – maybe he does.

The only thing that worried me slightly was when he talked about my cutting down the chemotherapy. Well, that's very tempting, but a hell of a decision to make. As far as I know, platinum chemotherapy is the only known killer of this particular cancer. But if anybody out there has found any alternative, please let me know. If not, then, horrendous as it is, I've got to carry on with it. Serlin did suggest the kinds of food that may help, and I'll pass them on for the benefit of anyone in a similar situation: yoghurt, honey and plenty of salads. But if you're like me you've probably had loads of advice about what you should eat – all conflicting. It's like having golf lessons from seven different players – you finish up twisting your neck, breaking your arm and falling over on your backside. But I am managing to keep some yoghurt and honey down today, which is a relief because this weight loss is terrifying.

Normally I'm pretty good at not getting depressed, but eventually it gets to you and I must say this is a very down time for me. I hope before this book ends it picks up, for your sake, because I don't want you to feel as bad as I do. It's hard now for me to believe that I'm the same person who was on *Wogan* at the end of 1990, so confident about everything and saying what a breeze it is to get over cancer. Well it's not – it's tough. I didn't know the meaning of the word before. What people go through when they have the other types of treatment I've no idea. Theirs goes on for months – they're constantly in hospital, day in, day out. I don't know how they cope. My son's partner has leukaemia and he has to make a decision about whether or not to have a massive operation. That's a hard thing to do. These people are so brave, and Ray rightly pointed out to me how lucky I am. It's a strange thing to say but I *am* lucky, exceedingly lucky. I mean, there are people with this illness who have to endure a lot more pain.

This second bout of cancer is the only time that I've actually thought about death, that I may actually be dying and about the consequences. I was speaking very deeply to Ray last week about that eventuality and sorting out my life, all the bits and bobs and practicalities that have to be seen to. I told him that when I go I don't want a funeral – I want a party. There was a programme on television called *The Foxes*, a great series;

when someone died they held a New Orleans-style funeral with a big celebration and a jazz band. That's what I want. That's the way I've lived, and that's the way I want to go if I've got to. I told him that I don't want any miseries – I want it to be a lot of fun, just like the way I lived. There were a lot of tears through our talk together and he told me not to think like that, and I suppose that's right. But it's got to be said – it's in my mind, in my heart. A part of me still thinks I'll win. I've still got so much to do.

My friends, both in and out of show business, have been a revelation to me since I've been ill. Tarbuck rings me two or three times a day to tell me jokes, Bob Monkhouse is always in contact and so too are Des O'Connor and Russ Conway. My friends Ray Stevens, Lou Manzie and David Mason couldn't have been more supportive. And the people who've written to me like Leslie Crowther, Denis Norden, Ernie Wise, Frankie Vaughan, Ronnie Corbett, the Beverley Sisters – the list is endless and I can't thank them enough. I know how scary even the word 'cancer' is to most people, so they've been wonderful to stick by me. I'll never forget any of them.

Peter Stringfellow is another one. He came to see me last night, even though I can't really talk much now. He told me that I've changed a lot through this illness and I think he's right. I seem to be sensible, more philosophical and more realistic. I've spent so much of my life worrying, mainly about my work, and it's only now that I realize how pointless all that is – after all, you can only be as good as you are, so it's crazy to stay awake at night paranoid about whether or not people like you. It's all superfluous – if they don't like you what are you going to do, you can only try your hardest and say, 'I'm sorry, I'm so sorry. I did the best I could.' But I spent years beating myself up about it. Now I think: well, if they want to pay me to come and work for them – fine. If not, it doesn't matter. If they don't like what I do, they can only sack me. If I go into another show one day, which I hope to do, I'll do my best and that's it. It's not that I don't care, just that my best is all I can give – no more worrying. The stars in my eyes have gone. I just want to be well and have a good life, to enjoy my friends and my family, and if the work is there then all well and good. If not, it's not the end of the world. For years and years I've hustled and worried, but those days have gone. They're over.

That's not to say I haven't loved it all. I just wish I'd been more sensible about it. When you're a young, strong performer your aim is to get to the top, and somewhere along the line you're an egomaniac. You have to be – you want stardom. No one goes into show business to be bottom of the heap. I wasn't any different, but success doesn't come to many and those who do make it to the heights are very talented, very fortunate and very determined. Very few have got to the pinnacle of our business without being very clever, very sensible and very hard. I wish I'd been more sensible, but I have been exceedingly lucky. I've been in showbiz for going on fifty years, I've topped the bill at the Palladium and had my own television shows, and you can't do a lot better than that. I'm also still working and still known. I reckon that in a way I've become a kind of institution given the amount of mail that I've had and the interest that's been shown over my well-being in the last six months – it's been incredible and very gratifying. I've loved it all and I want to carry on loving it, and I'm not ashamed to say that I like the notoriety that goes with it as well. I do like to go to Langan's and get service, or to Tramp or Stringfellows and get champagne and cuddles on the table. Yes, I do – and long may I continue. Maybe if I handle myself right from now on and don't push and scratch it will do.

It's taken me a long time to realize what's important; but now I'm back with my brother, I have wonderful friends and a family which defies description – they've been so caring and loving to me. My wife has tried so hard to look after me and help me get better and she's been so strong for me. How can I possibly thank her for that, and how can I possibly tell her how sorry I am for the times that I've misbehaved and hurt her in our life together? I've done some incredibly stupid things which now I regret deeply. I wish I hadn't. And Ray – well, just to think about him brings tears to my eyes. He's been my friend, my son, my right-hand man – what can I say? He's a better son than I deserve. I know it's a fact of life that you can't live forever but I've too many reasons for not wanting to go yet, too much life still to live, too many things to do and too many experiences to have. A part of me still thinks I'll beat this cancer and you'll know this by the end of the book: if it isn't finished, you'll know we lost and it'll end very abruptly, but I promise I'll try to finish it. I've just got to get a little better . . . .

14

In Siggi's Words

Bernie grew thinner and weaker over the next ten days, until by Easter Monday we had to take him back to the Clinic. As well as not being able to eat he had become dehydrated: he was unable even to swallow fluid. He had developed a bad chest pain from the chemotherapy, and it was that which was preventing him from swallowing. As soon as he arrived at the Clinic, he was put on a drip, and after a few days he started to feel stronger to the point where he was bossing the nurses around again and could get up to shave and wash himself. After a week the doctors gave him the good news that his liver had shrunk back quite well and that his blood count was good. That really bucked him up and he said, 'There! Told you I'd beat it.' But he was still unable to swallow, so a tube was put through his nose to feed him. He found that uncomfortable and did not want anybody to see him looking like that.

He stayed in hospital for three weeks this time, even longer than when he'd had his stomach operation, and by the last week he desperately wanted to come home. He was told that he wouldn't be allowed out until he could drink two pints of fluid a day, and I've never seen him try so hard to do anything in his life. We finally brought him home on Saturday 20 April, and he was so happy to be there with his dogs and family that Ray and I believed for a while that he might pull through. He was so strong and positive, saying that although when he was in hospital he'd thought that he wouldn't be coming home again, when he was finally there he felt much more optimistic. He told us, 'I've beaten it before and I'm going to beat it again. My liver's okay, my blood's okay. All I have to do now is get stronger. I'm going to go for walks with the dogs, go on holiday, and start all over again.' By the afternoon he was very tired and went to bed.

What Bernie never knew was that right from the time of his operation in August 1990 Ray and I had been keeping a terrible secret. We'd known all along that he was going to die. The doctors had told us that the cancer had already spread from his stomach to his liver and that eventually it would kill him. They said at the time that he could have another five years left to live, and Ray and I determined that he would never know how ill he really was. He'd always said that he wouldn't want to know when he was going to die, and he never asked the doctors the question: 'How long have I got?' He seemed to avoid that, even though he would ask how well he was doing or if the chemotherapy was working. Bernie was so brave, a hero, and couldn't believe that the illness could take his body over so much and that he couldn't do anything about it. Ray and I realized that we couldn't tell anyone else: not even his closest friends or my mother, Mike or Bernie's sister Sylvia. We dreaded the possibility that somebody might let it slip and that Bernie would just give up and stop fighting for his life.

It was hard to live with such a lie. Sometimes we found that Bernie would ask us the strangest questions, trying to find out if we knew more than we were admitting while at the same time not really wanting to know. He was a very intelligent man and we were fully aware that a wrong look or remark that didn't make sense to him could give away our secret. We found ourselves having to cover our tracks very precisely. If I told Bernie something while Ray wasn't there I'd have to alert him so that he would say something similar. Sometimes I found that I could get away with it as his wife by telling him off and bullying him. I would say, 'Stop complaining about being tired. You're better now.' This was so normal to him that by the end he was calling me 'Siggi Schwarzkopf' or 'Stormin' Siggi', after the American general who commanded the Allied forces in the Gulf War. So I knew that I could keep the truth from him but didn't dare tell anyone else. Some of Bernie's friends, I know, thought I was being over-protective, but a wrong glance or reaction from them would have told Bernie everything in an instant. He was able to read the people closest to him like a book. Some may have recognized from their own experience that Bernie was in a critical condition, but that would still have only been speculation on their part.

I was frightened, as well, that others might shy away from him completely at a time when he needed them most. He got a lot of strength from joking with people, making plans and normal events like being invited out to dinner, even though we had to refuse. While he was making plans he felt he had a future – in fact he had already booked himself up to do pantomime for Christmas 1991, and even when he was in hospital and had to miss a personal appearance he said he hoped he'd be asked again. He passed the job on to Lionel Blair, who promised that in return he'd buy him dinner when he came out of hospital. His whole attitude was that of a man who was determined to be well again, and I didn't want to do anything that would stop him feeling that way.

Ray was incredibly strong during this time, and I leaned on him a lot. When the doctors first said that Bernie's cancer was incurable I remember that we left the Clinic in a daze and eventually went into a pub. Ray never drinks, but he ordered a bourbon and downed it in one gulp and then bought drinks for everyone at the bar. I asked him what he was doing but he really didn't know. It was his way of screaming, I suppose.

There was a time in October 1990 when I really believed that the doctors had got it wrong. Our friend Ray Stevens had lent us his villa in Spain, and although Bernie was still due to have more chemotherapy he seemed so healthy out there. He ate and swam and enjoyed the sunshine, and I thought all the doctors were bonkers. Then before he started in pantomime we took a holiday in Nassau. He'd been very choosy about where we should go, rejecting Miami because there'd be too many people on the beach to see how thin he was, and passing up Barbados because the television was no good there. We had a glorious time. Bernie took a selection of plays on video to watch and we'd lie on the beach playing Scrabble, eating hamburgers and drinking beer. The world was wonderful – just like old times. In the afternoon he'd go back to the hotel room to have a nap or watch TV, but for the first time in months he had neither pain nor medication. He didn't even mind when some English people on the beach recognized him and mentioned that he'd lost weight: he told them quite proudly that he'd beaten cancer.

It was almost as much of a shock to me as it was to Bernie when he became ill again. On the Thursday morning after he'd come out of hospital he was in pain again and couldn't drink. Before then he'd managed to swallow a little soup and he would say, 'Tomorrow I'll have twice as much and then I'll put weight back on again.' But now it was clear he was becoming dehydrated.

On the day that we had to take him back to the Clinic, I knew he would not come home again. I phoned Ray, who came straight over instead of going to work. Bernie was watching television and Ray lay down beside him on the bed and fell asleep. His way of coping with his father's dying was to over-eat, and he had put on quite a lot of weight. There was a programme on television about baby elephants and Bernie and I laughed when we saw our son lying there snoring, looking for all the world like one of them.

While Bernie dozed I was able to hold his hand and tell him I loved him very much and whisper goodbye. Later on he returned to the Clinic for the last time. I couldn't travel with them in the ambulance. Instead I took my own car, explaining to Bernie that I would follow on with his night clothes.

For a couple of days he seemed stronger again, still full of hope and determination. Ray moved into the hospital, only leaving to buy the odd snack. Then Bernie started to get very tired and by the Saturday had fallen into a deep sleep. Ray sat with him day and night, talking to him, singing songs and making plans. Sometimes we really believed that Bernie could hear us: he seemed to respond with a movement of his foot or flutter of his eyes. I would drive to the hospital in the morning and sit with him for a while, reading out all the cards and messages he'd been sent. Then I'd drive to the shops. I didn't know what I was doing there and I kept buying pairs of tights. I bought hundreds of pairs of tights: I don't know why. Ray told me I shouldn't be driving, but it seemed to be the only thing that was keeping me sane.

It didn't seem possible, but Bernie lost even more weight: another four stone in all. He was literally fading away. It was heartbreaking to see his frail body when the nurse changed his clothes. I'm sure one day I even saw a doctor crying as he left the room because he couldn't help him. Bernie still seemed to be fighting so hard for his life. On Thursday afternoon I told him to let go. I don't know if he heard me. At five minutes to eight on Saturday morning, 4 May, he died.

I don't remember much about that day. The radio had given the news and the phone never stopped ringing. I know that I tried to tell the dogs that their Daddy wouldn't be coming home any more, and they seemed to understand.

Everybody – strangers and friends – has been very kind with their messages and letters of sympathy. The thing Bernie loved most in life was making people laugh, and I know that he wouldn't want us to mope now. He tried very hard to finish this book because he wanted people to know it was worth fighting against cancer. So just because he's not with us any more it doesn't mean to say that anyone with the disease should give up. They must carry on fighting, because at least that can help prolong their life. A friend of ours came up to me at Bernie's funeral to tell me that his mother had had four extra months of life after hearing Bernie say that he'd fought stomach cancer and beaten it. Apparently she'd said that if Bernie could do it, so could she!

I would like to thank everybody who has written to me; I'd had no idea how much Bernie was loved. I still can't believe that he's gone, but once upon a long time ago, he told me he would always be with me. So if you can hear me, Bernie, I love you, and so too do a lot of other people out there.

IN LOVING MEMORY

DES O'CONNOR

Bernie was one of my oldest and closest friends in show business. Our friendship spanned thirty years and during that time we worked together on countless occasions and socialised regularly. We shared so many happy and funny experiences together and I can really say that he touched my life in a major way. I know that in his autobiography he tells of the occasion when I flew out to Spain to present Siggi and him with a long-service medal to mark their wedding anniversary. Their own double act really was something special. I have also known Ray since he was a baby and I was delighted to be one of the guests at his wedding last year. It was a marvellous occasion and Bernie was in great form. During his speech at the reception he turned to his new daughter-in-law and said, 'Tina, now that you are part of the family, you no longer need to call my wife Mrs Winters. Call her by her real name – Hitler!'

Bernie was warm, generous and a naturally funny man and I shall miss his friendship greatly.

SU POLLARD

Bernie had more bubble and squeak than Sainsbury's. He

was a lovely man and a delight to work with. We became great mates when we performed in panto together at the Richmond Theatre in 1988. It was Dick Whittington – I was Dick and Bernie, ably assisted by Schnorbitz, played Widow Twanky.

One of the best things about working on stage with Bernie was the great fun we used to have together ad-libbing as situations would occur. However, my favourite memory from the panto involves the night Schnorbitz upstaged both of us. There was a particular scene in which the Alderman, played by Ken Bruce, would accuse me of stealing a bracelet and banish me from London. At this point Bernie would jump to my defence and threaten to set Schnorbitz on him. However, on this occasion, Bernie couldn't believe his eyes when Schnorbitz actually took one step towards Ken, slowly rolled on to her back with her feet in the air and remained in that position for the rest of the scene. The cast and audience all broke up and no one laughed louder than Bernie.

He had genuine charisma and it was a real privilege to work with such a great talent and a lovely man.

PHILIP JONES

In a moving and affectionate tribute at Bernie Winters' funeral Bob Monkhouse said that for him Bernie was still alive.

That is how I feel. I can see Bernie with astonishing clarity and am grateful to have known and worked for thirty years with quite the nicest and warmest comic in the business.

He and Mike worked an extraordinarily demanding schedule in the sixties and seventies, often playing two TV series, a summer season and a pantomime in each year. One year they were in summer season in Yarmouth and each Saturday night after the second house they crossed the Pennines in a light aircraft to be in Blackpool for Sunday's live TV show.

Bernie was a great and natural comic. But for me it was his warmth and vulnerability which were his most endearing qualities. As with all clowns, tears were never far from laughter for Bernie. He cried on the last night of a TV show singing 'Bye, Bye, Blackpool' to the tune of 'Bye Bye, Blackbird'. Appearing with the legendary Sophie Tucker one night in 1964 was almost too much for him; and he could never restrain the tears when appearing as Bud Flanagan singing those nostalgic songs.

He was, in other words, sincere in his approach to show business and, above all, he cared.

Bob Monkhouse quoted John O'Hara who, on being told of George Gershwin's death said, 'I don't have to believe it if I don't want to'. Quite the nicest thing to say about anyone and that is how I feel about Bernie Winters.

Philip Jones was Bernie's first TV producer and Head of Light Entertainment at Thames Television for twenty years.

LESLIE CROWTHER

As a man to tour with, Bernie was beautiful but eccentric. He kept very late hours and as his touring partner in *Bud 'n' Ches* I had to keep pace with him. There are two incidents in Belfast which aptly describe the way he led the charge. We were appearing at the Opera House and after the show one night we were invited to the opening of an Italian restaurant by the local police. Their involvement only became apparent when we arrived at the restaurant. It was obvious that they were keeping an eye out for any local mafia-type disturbances. We were taken into a private room upstairs in the restaurant and halfway through the spaghetti it became obvious that there was an altercation occurring downstairs in the main restaurant. The police force thundered down the stairs – Bernie and I crept down after them and beheld what looked like a very badly acted bar-room brawl in a Hollywood 'B' cowboy feature. Immediately assuming our well-known impersonation of cowering dogs we crawled out between the legs of the fighters and reached the street where we stood up and watched people being carried out by the score. I wouldn't mind but we missed the dessert.

This incident happened in 1982 and on the way over from Ayr in Scotland, Bernie asked me on the plane how I proposed to visit the Irish National Trust properties which I had expressed the desire to case during our three weeks in Northern Ireland. I said, 'I've no idea, I presume I'll have to hire a car.' Bernie with a knowing wink said '. . . leave it to your Jewish friend.'

When we arrived in Belfast we were immediately whisked off to Ulster Television for an interview. The interviewer asked us what we planned to do with our spare time during the day. Bernie explained we had no car – and within five minutes the studio switchboard was inundated with offers of free vehicles. Bernie chose a rather nice saloon car and I selected a farm jeep which had recently been used for muck spreading. The farmer had cleaned it out prior to giving it to me. The wonderful generosity of these Irish people would not have been possible had not Bernie dropped a fairly obvious hint on the telly. He was a lovely man and I shall miss him.

JIMMY TARBUCK

I knew Bernie for nearly thirty years and loved him dearly. He was one of those people who genuinely lit up a room when he walked into it. Bernie was a great performer – a real clown. I think that if he had been American he would have been a great comedy film star – another Jerry Lewis, perhaps. He was great fun to perform with as well. When he was on *Live From Her Majesty's* with me, he just didn't want to finish our spot together and cheekily told the musical director that Englebert Humperdinck – who was top of the bill – could drop a song instead in order that we could carry on with our act!

I remember more than twenty years ago his great excitement when he bought his first American car – a maroon and white Chevrolet. He took me down the promenade to Blackpool pleasure beach and let me drive it back again. I had never come across power brakes before and when I touched them, the car screeched to a halt and Bernie shot off his seat and completely disappeared under the dashboard. Absolutely on cue a policeman walked up to the car. 'Is this yours, sir?' he asked. 'No, no, no,' I said. 'It's his,' pointing to an empty seat next to me. We hadn't drunk a thing, I promise.

Bernie was always so warm and generous and such fun to be with. I will miss him enormously.

CILLA BLACK

It was a pleasure to know such a lovely man as Bernie. He was one of the kindest and most warm-hearted men in the business. Whenever I was with him he'd have me doubled up with laughter. I'll miss him a lot.

LIONEL BLAIR

I've known Bernie almost all my life and loving him is like losing a brother to me. I loved him dearly and will miss him enormously.

One of my favourite memories of Bernie is when we were rehearsing *Big Night Out* for ABC Television. He and Mike were doing a sketch in which Mike kept telling him he'd had enough of working with him and wanted to go solo. The trouble was that every time they rehearsed it Bernie would burst into tears. When it came to the actual performance, Bernie didn't know how he was going to look angry rather than sad. The only solution we could think of was to hold a picture of Adolf Hitler in front of him . . . it worked!

PETE MURRAY

I knew Bernie Winters for thirty-four years. We were together on the *6.5 Special* TV show and remained firm friends for all that time. I can remember when we were doing the show in Cardiff both he and his brother Mike were joining me for dinner afterwards. Eventually they turned up late and made their apologies. They were held up because of the visiting Spanish football team – both being dark it was assumed that they were members of the side and were sitting down to have dinner with them!

For years I tried to persuade Bernie to branch out as an actor. In 1984 this was realised. We toured the country in Neil Simon's *The Odd Couple*. Bernie played the role created by Walter Matthau – Walter would have been proud of him!

Whilst on tour we played a lot of golf. Very badly. I remember at Billingham Bernie lost five balls on the first tee. Then at the end of the game he claimed he had won, until, that is, I reminded him of the lost balls on the first tee.

Eight weeks before Bernie passed away, he telephoned me. 'Pete, I hear you have lost your golf clubs. Can I help?'

'Bernie,' I replied, 'you're too ill, don't worry about clubs!'

Well, he did worry, and through the auspices of Cresta Sports a superb set of bag and clubs were delivered to me. I telephoned Bernie to thank him. 'Are they all right, Pete?' he enquired.

'All right, Bernie? I replied. 'All right? I love you.' And I did and always will and I miss him like mad.

MAURICE LEONARD

I worked with Bernie making twenty editions a year of the game show *Whose Baby?* for Thames Television between 1986 and 1988. He was a lovely man to work with and gave his all to the show. I got to know Siggi and Ray, too, during this time and even his mother-in-law who became the butt of many of Bernie's jokes, despite the fact that he adored her.

I remember when Chay Blyth, the yachtsman, was a guest on the show and was recounting an incident during one of his adventures where he spent thirty hours in shark-infested waters under his upturned boat. There was a sharp intake of breath from the studio audience as they pictured the incredible danger Chay must have faced. Suddenly Bernie piped up, 'You should have had my mother-in-law with you – she's the best shark repellent in the business!'

It was a pleasure to work with Bernie and the world of show business will be distinctly poorer for his loss.

PETER STRINGFELLOW

Bernie was not just a friend, he was a very dear friend and one of the nicest men I have ever met. Whilst we did not live in each other's pockets, we always found time to meet up somewhere along the line, usually by accident.

This is a story which I think is typical of Bernie.

Mike and Bernie used to play for me in the early seventies at one of my cabaret clubs in Leeds called Rockerfellas, and they were a very big name act in those days. I used to drink a lot more than I should, and certainly more than I do now, and we would play poker every night. I thought I was a bit of a 'hotshot' and it used to baffle me that whilst he was as drunk as I was neither of us used to end up losing by the end of the night, or should I say the morning. We met up many times over the years and always ended up playing poker. With Bernie playing, everything was a joke; he found everything funny, which suited me. By the eighties I realized I was a lousy poker player for though I never lost to Bernie, I never won anything from him either.

It was only after Bernie's death that I was told by his brother Mike that Bernie was an expert poker player. They had both been taught by their father who was a professional gambler and Mike and Bernie could clear the table of every penny if they so wished. So for all those years Bernie had been playing around with me, letting me think he was an inept player like myself. We had a tremendous amount of fun and he never took a pound off me: that is what I call a nice fella and a good friend!

INDEX